WHAT I HEAR WHEN GOD SPEAKS

WHAT I HEAR
WHEN GOD SPEAKS

ALLEN BROWN

What I Hear When God Speaks

Copyright © 2019 by Allen Brown. All rights reserved.

No part of this publication may be reproduced, stored in a retrieval system or transmitted in any way by any means, electronic, mechanical, photocopy, recording or otherwise without the prior permission of the author except as provided by USA copyright law.

This novel is a work of fiction. Names, descriptions, entities, and incidents included in the story are products of the author's imagination. Any resemblance to actual persons, events, and entities is entirely coincidental.

The opinions expressed by the author are not necessarily those of URLink Publishing.

1603 Capitol Ave., Suite 310 Cheyenne, Wyoming USA 82001
1-888-980-6523 | admin@urlinkpublishing.com

URLink Publishing is committed to excellence in the publishing industry.

Book design copyright © 2018 by URLink Publishing. All rights reserved.

Published in the United States of America

ISBN 978-1-64753-004-4 (Paperback)
ISBN 978-1-64753-003-7 (Digital)

19.10.19

CONTENTS

Introduction 7
A Comparison of the Five Wills 9
A Son Came into the Light Because of Love 15
A Specific Set of Love. 24
A Spiritual Beginning 29
A Tingling Spiritual Trinity The Trinitarian God. 34
Adam, God's Created Son,
Was Not God's Born-Again Son. 40
The Anointed Ones 46
Before I Became Flesh, I Was the Created
Image of God Guided by the Will of God!. 49
Belief, Believe, and the Believer
By Faith in Jesus Christ. 54
Conscious Life. 55
Created without Sin, Adam? 58
Creator, Redeemer, and Revealer God is Jesus Christ . . 64
Faith Is the Body of Holiness 67
From a Seed to a Tree 71
God Created Satan, Satan Created Sin,
God Created Us 76
God Has a Time and Date for All of Us. 82
God, the Good and Great Farmer. 86

God Trust Us	90
God's Plan	95
How Long Is Eternity	100
I Am to Become the Invisible Image of God	105
I Shall Recover It All with Faith	108
I Would Not Be If It Were Not for God	112
In Us (Trust), Through Us (Runs Faith), and Out of Us (the Transformation)	117
Looking for the Wisdom of God	122
Love Creates, Hate Destroys	125
Love is the Life That We Live	132
Man is the Set Head	135
What God Has Done for Me My Soul Is Where God's Spirit Lives	137
To Whom Much Is Given, Much Is Required	140
Of Whom I Speak, He Is the Beginning	146
One Mind One Goal, One Body, One Soul	153
Our Fight Is Not with Each Other	157
Out of the Soul of Man Comes the Light of the Lord	163
Perfection—the Number Three	171
Reality Check	177
Soul, Body, Spirit Versus the Father, the Son. and the Holy Ghost	181
Sons of God	185
Stones of Fire Revealed	190
The Brain is Carnal, the Mind is Spiritual	192
The Crown of Creation	195

INTRODUCTION

These stories are the conversations discussed and talked about by God and myself within my personal relationship with God. Through these conversations is how I have come to understand that God is my Lord Jesus the Christ. The Holy Ghost has revealed to me that Christ is who that was with God in the beginning as the Word. The Word is the Seed and Egg of God. These two are the Father, and the Holy Ghost that constitutes the Christ, the Power and Wisdom of God, for God is the Word, the Father and Mother of himself. It is the Word that created darkness and formed light, this light is the image of God, the Righteous One who is all: Light. It is by the Power and Wisdom of God that this is done. This power and wisdom is the Christ, called the Spiritual Son of God. The Father, the Power of God, was sent to earth by the Wisdom of God, the Holy Ghost, to the woman named Mary, and Jesus was born, the savior of the world. This child is the possessor of all the power and wisdom of God; this child is Life. These stories are what I have learned from my talking to God. I am blessed because of them, and I hope my readers are too. In the name of our Lord Jesus Christ, I thank you.

A COMPARISON OF THE FIVE WILLS

A thought occurred to me—out of the darkness came the light, and out of God the creation of Satan was conceived.

"Why," I asked my Lord, "why was Satan created?"

The Spirit revealed that he was created to be a guardian angel.

> Thou art the anointed cherub that covereth; and I have set thee so: thou wast upon the holy mountain of God; thou hast walked up and down in the mist of the stones of fire. (Ezek. 28:14)

This scripture is saying that God created and blessed Satan as a guardian angel. God ordained him to be a mighty angelic guardian. We, as men with faith in the Lord Jesus Christ, sin will not be held against us.

> Blessed is he whose transgression is forgiven, whose sin is covered. (Ps. 32:1, KJV)

This is not true for Satan. He chose to sin against God to prove to creation that he would rise above the stars of God. Satan lied to creation and said that he would become like God. How could this be true if God himself created Satan? Five times Satan has lied to creation by saying *I will*.

> For thou hast said in thine heart, "*I will* ascend into heaven, *I will* exalt my throne above the stars of God: *I will* sit also upon the mount of the Congregation, in the sides of the north: *I will* ascend above the heights of the clouds; *I will* be like the Most High." (Isa. 14:13–14; italics added)

The five "I wills" of Satan were not of the will of God. These were the five iniquities Satan had in his heart against God.

> Thou wast perfect in thy ways from the day that thou wast created, till iniquity was found in thee. (Ezek. 28:15)

So again I say, how could Satan's lie to all creation—I will be like God—be true if God created him. Satan failed at what God created him to be because of the five wicked, evil, and sinful ways that were found in him. Because of the failures of Satan, God created man in His own image. Because of the creation of man, Satan's iniquities have become hatred toward God and man. The wickedness that God found in Satan caused him to kick Satan out from his place among the stones of fire.

> How art thou fallen from heaven, O Lucifer, son of the morning! How art thou cut down to the ground, which didst weaken the nations? (Isa. 14:12)

With each creation, there are nations within that creation that wait for the commands of God's will for their nation. God commands all of creation. There are different angelic beings as well as different angelic nations in heaven as there are different races of people. There are different countries. There are different nations on the earth.

The fall of Satan weakened the nations by dividing the perception of how powerful God was. God is all-powerful. Satan seeked to become more powerful than God. Satan lies to all of the nations in creation, and he lies to men and to the nations of men. Because of the wickedness of Satan, sin entered the world.

> Wherefore, as by one man sin entered into the world and death by sin; and so death passed upon all men, for that all have sinned: for until the law sin was in the world: but sin is not imputed when there is no law. (Rom. 5:12–13, KJV)

By the use of sin, the same five iniquities God found in Satan before God created man.

Here in Ezekiel 28:15, God is speaking about Satan.

> Thou wast perfect in thy ways from the day that thou wast created, till iniquity was found in thee.

Satan was created before man and sinned. Satan was the one who brought sin into the world. This is the reason God placed man in the garden, to isolate him from the sin that was already in the world.

> And the Lord God planted a garden eastward in Eden; and there he put the man whom he had formed. (Gen. 2:8, KJV)

We, as children of God, are not to allow our nature to be corrupted by the five iniquities of Satan's will. We are to be guided by the five "I wills" found in Jeremiah 31:33–34. This scripture refers to God's will for our lives.

> "But this shall be the covenant that *I will* make with the house of Israel; After those days, saith the Lord, *I will* put my law in their inward parts, and write it in their hearts; and *I will* be their God, and they shall be my people. And they shall teach no more every man his neighbor, and every man

his brother, saying, Know the Lord: for they shall all know me, from the least of them unto the greatest of them, saith the Lord: "for *I will* forgive their iniquity, and *I will* remember their sin no more." (italics added)

The five "I wills" of God are in short,

1. *I will* make them my people.
2. *I will* put My word in their hearts.
3. *I will* be their God.
4. *I will* forgive their wickedness.
5. *I will* remember their sins no more.

Satan is always trying to use the flip side of his lies to distort God as being the one true God.

See the truth of God like the number nine. There are three number threes in the number nine . The lie of Satan would make the number nine look like the number six flipped upside down. The truth about the number six is there are only two threes in it. This means two things—one, Satan, two, lies.

Whereas the nine has three threes that represent, one, the Father, two, the Son, and three, the Holy Spirit.

This is why God is the truth shown upright as the number nine.

You can see the number of perfection in the number nine—three times as three is divided by nine revealing the order of God's perfection.

The Father holds the time in His hands (past, present and future).

The Son is the door we go through or space (width, height, and depth).

The Holy Spirit is he who makes our hearts feel like concrete or matter (atom, neutron, and protons).

All nine of these elements add up to God's created universe. God created this creation of perfection out of nothing but himself.

This is to glorify God.

Amen!

A SON CAME INTO THE LIGHT BECAUSE OF LOVE

> Verily, verily, I say unto you, The hour is coming, and now is, when the dead shall hear the voice of the Son of God: and they that hear shall live.
>
> —John 5:25 (KJV)

Jesus died and was resurrected; this was God's will showing his love for his Son, as well as for his children. When Jesus died, Jesus stepped into the darkness—hell. When Jesus came out of darkness, he was brought out of hell by the power of God through resurrection, and so are the children of God.

It is also stated in verse 29 that

> And shall come forth; they that have done good, unto the resurrection of life; and they that have done evil, unto the resurrection of damnation.

The children of God are to come out of the darkness of sin using their faith within Jesus Christ, the door way to the presence of God. This was done spiritually by the children's faith in Christ Jesus. Jesus Christ is declared the Son of God.

The scripture speaks of this in Romans 1:4 (KJV),

> And declared to be the Son of God with power, according to the Spirit of holiness, by the resurrection from the dead.

God created his Son to walk into darkness and to walk out of the same darkness because of love. God has great love for his Son, the world, and for his children—Adam and Eve. God so loved the world because this was where God planted the seeds of man to became the adopted bornagain children of God.

The Bible says that God so loved the world.

> For God so loved the world, that he gave his only begotten Son, that whosoever believeth in him should not perish, but have everlasting life. (John 3:16, KJV)

Adam had a God-given right to choose of his own free will to obey or not to obey the command God gave him. The Bible speaks of this command in Genesis 2:17 (KJV) which says,

> But of the tree of the knowledge of good and evil, thou shalt not eat of it: for in the day that thou eatest thereof thou shalt surely die.

God knows all. This is why Adam was given a free will— "For in the day that thou eatest, this is revealed to mean that, when you chose to eat, you will surely die."

God reveals what would happen to Adam. This was that command.

What is a command?

According to the *Random House College Dictionary*, a command is an order given by a person in authority.

God had authority over Adam.

God created him.

> So God created man in his own image, in the image of God created he him; male and female created he them. (Gen. 1:27, KJV)

God gave Adam free will. God gave Adam the right to choose. The Spirit reveals this to me in Genesis 4:7 (KJV) that

> If thou doest well, shalt thou not be accepted? And if thou doest not well, sin lieth at the door. And unto thee shall be his desire, and thou shalt rule over him.

This was a choice.

Adam had the right to believe or not to believe that God would redeem him and make him a born-again child of God. God gave Adam his Spirit, not the spirit of fear.

> Hereby know we that we dwell in him, and he in us, because he hath given us of his Spirit. (1 John 4:13, KJV)

Here the gift of God's spirit is revealed as being given. Adam chose to believe God's will for his life. It is God's will for his created people to become his born-again children. God wants us to become born of him.

Without sin, how would being born again be possible?

In the beginning God created Lucifer with sin in him.

> Thou wast perfect in thy ways from the day that thou wast created, till iniquity was found in thee. (Ezek. 28:15, KJV)

What was found in him was created in him by God. God knew that Lucifer would come for man. This was all God's plan—to teach man who he was and how to become born again. We are to learn how to walk out of sin into the light of God.

> For God who commanded the light to shine out of darkness, hath shined in our hearts, to

> give the light of the knowledge of the glory of God in the face of Jesus Christ. (2 Cor. 4:6, kjv)

God had this plan that man would grow out of sin and would become the child of God.

> But ye are a chosen generation, a royal priesthood, a holy nation, a peculiar people; that ye should show forth the praise of him who hath called you out of darkness into his marvelous light. (1 Pet. 2:9, kjv)

(God's plan, this is revealed, by the Holy Spirit.)

The Son does the will of God because it was God's command. This is possible because this Son, the second Adam, came from heaven.

> The first man is of the earth, earthy: the second man is the Lord from heaven. (1 Cor. 15:47, kjv)

The adopted child, the true believer, chooses to love God because of the love that God has for the child. Not that the child loves God, but the child comes to know God's love for himself and decides to love God by accepting Jesus Christ as his redeemer.

Herein is love, not that we loved God, but that he loved us, and sent his Son to be the propitiation for our sins. (1 John 4:10, KJV)

It was because of the love God had for Adam that Adam chose to disobey. The love of God is so great it could only be understood through the test of sin. This is why God created his Son to walk into sin and walk back out of the same sin because of love, which is God.

1 John 4:8 (KJV) says,

> He that loveth not knoweth not God; for God is love.

Lucifer was created with iniquity in him, for this purpose, to give birth to sin. Sin was used to steer man back into the presence of God. Sin was a gift to Lucifer to use against man.

The way Lucifer got sin in man is told in Genesis 3:6 (KJV).

> And when the woman saw that the tree was good for food, and that it was pleasant to the eyes, and a tree to be desired to make one wise, she took of the fruit thereof, and did eat, and gave also unto her husband with her; and he did eat.

This was not a blatant disobedience but a well-thoughtout decision created by God for the free will of

Adam. So the Spirit reveals! This is the word of God. Adam's disobedience was made with the God given right, free will. It was determined with the wisdom of God that was given him in the image of God he was created in. The image of God he was created in gave Adam the mind of God.

> And out of the ground the Lord God formed every beast of the field, and every fowl of the air, and brought them unto Adam to see what he would call them: and whatsoever Adam called every living creature, that was the name thereof. (Gen. 2:9, KJV)

This was proven to Adam when he named all of the animals. It showed Adam knew the things of God. Spiritually Adam had the mind of God. God asked Adam their names (not as if he didn't know their names). This was to reveal to Adam that he had the mind of God.

1 Corinthians 2:16 (KJV) says,

> Foe who hath known the mind of the Lord, that he may instruct him? But we have the mind of Christ.

Christ is the power of God in the flesh. The mind of Christ was in Adam. Adam was the created son of God. He was not born of God. Jesus was the second Adam who was born of God. It is through Jesus that we are born again and are made children. Jesus Christ was God's plan to redeem Adam, the first Adam. As Christ rose, all of mankind would be redeemed. Those that were born and died and lived according to God's will before Jesus was born will also be redeemed. This was God's plan for man—that men would become his born-again children.

The Spirit reveals this as the truth in Romans 8:16 (KJV) which states that

> The Spirit itself beareth witness with our spirit, that we are the children of God.

Awesome.

This is so true.

God stepped out of eternity into time, into darkness, to reveal to mankind who he really is, and how much God really loves us. God became a child that we might personally know him through faith.

> And we know that the Son of God is come, and hath given us an understanding, that we may know him that is true, and we are in him that is true, even in his Son Jesus Christ. This is the true God, and eternal life. (1 John 5:20, KJV)

The Son stepped in and out of darkness because of love. This Son, the Lord God, the one true God, our God, Christ.

Jesus Christ!
Stepped out of darkness!
Stepped into the light!
The loving light of God!

This is to glorify God!

A SPECIFIC SET OF LOVE

> Israel, I will make you my wife forever.
> I will be honest and faithful to you. I will show you my love and compassion.
> —Hosea 2:19
> (GOD'S WORD translation [gw])

Israel is God's chosen people, the people God gave his love too. There is a specific set of love that the Lord God has given us all. This is the set of love created for us by our Lord God.

> So the Lord God caused him to fall into a deep sleep. While the man was sleeping, the Lord God took out one of the man's ribs and closed up the flesh at that place. Then the Lord God formed a woman from the rib that he had taken from the man. He brought her to the man. (Gen. 2:21–22, gw)

This is the creation of the specific set of love. The love of God manifested in Adam for Eve is the first specific love, and the love of God manifested in Eve for Adam is the second specific love.

Adam and Eve was brought together by God. They were of one flesh.

> This is now bone of my bones, and flesh of my flesh. She will be named woman because she was taken from man. (Gen. 2:23, GW)

This set is given to each one of us individually. There is the love of God in a woman or man chosen by God for you. This is the love, I believe, we should be looking for or waiting for. The love of God is in your woman or in your man.

It says in the 1 John 4:12 (GW) that

> No one has ever seen God. If we love each other, God lives in us, and his love is perfected in us.

This is the love God has willed for us to fall in love with, Him—the love of God.

For God is Love.

Verse 16 of the same chapter states that

> We have known and believed that God loves us. God is love. Those who live in God's love live in God, and God lives in them.

We are to love God. This is because God's love is in other people for us. This love of God's is Spiritual. A specific set of love, spiritually, is one spirit, and physically, it is two people in love with the love of God. These two people are male and female.

In the beginning this love begins with Adam, and out of Adam came Eve. These two people were of the same flesh and spirit.

> That is why a man will leave his father and mother and will be united with his wife, and they will become one flesh. (Gen. 2:24, GW)

The flesh houses the Spirit—the Spirit of God. This is so because in the beginning God created Adam who God gave His own Spirit and image of Love to.

The Bible says that God created man in his own image.

> So God created humans in his image. In the image of God he created them. He created them male and female. (Gen. 1:27, GW)

God brought Eve out of Adam. This is why they share the same Spirit. God is the Spirit of love. It is this love that we are in love with—God. It is not the physical aspects of the woman or the man that we love (things we like), but it is the love of God in the woman or man we should fall in love with.

> So love the Lord your God with all your heart, with all your soul, with all your mind, and with all your strength. (Mark 12:30, GW)

This same love of God is equally given between two people, to share God's love with one another while they're here on earth. Spiritually, in the eyes of God, they are one Spirit (in the likeness of Adam and Eve, a specific set of love). We, that are saved, share the same Spirit.

> Now, we didn't receive the spirit that belongs to the world. Instead, we received the Spirit who comes from God so that we could know the things which God has freely given us. (1 Cor. 2:12, GW)

This Spirit is the Spirit of God, the Holy Ghost. It is this Spirit that teaches us who we should fall in love with. The Holy Ghost knows who the other part of us is, the other person that God has chosen for us to love.

> Wherefore as the Holy Ghost saith, Today if ye will hear his voice. (Heb. 3:7, GW)

The voice of the Spirit reveals that this is the person we are to fall in love with, and the Spirit lives in that person that God has chosen for us. This is the love we long for. I myself, I long to be in love with the love of God that is in my specific woman. She has the specific love of God in herself for me.

That is the kind of woman I am going to marry to glorify the name of the Lord God. Amen.

This is and will always be to glorify God!

A SPIRITUAL BEGINNING

> I write unto you, little children, because your sins are forgiven you for his name's sake.
> —1 John 2:12 (KJV)

Life is lived in and out of the Flesh.
Living life in the flesh is physical.
Galatians 2:20 says,

> I am crucified with Christ: nevertheless I live; yet not I, but Christ liveth in me: and the life which I now live in the flesh I live by the faith of the Son of God, who loved me, and gave himself for me.

Living life out of the flesh is spiritual.

> That which was from the beginning, which we have heard, which we have seen with our eyes, which we have looked upon, and our hands have handled, of the Word of life. (1 John 1:1)

Who is living the life?

The three images of God, the Father, the Son and the Holy Ghost—also us as the true believers.

The physical and the spiritual. These two aspects are at war, and the war is being fought in the mind.

Romans 7:23 says,

> But I see another law in my members, warring against the law of my mind, and bringing me into captivity to the law of sin which is in my members.

Who is the mind? (This is the answer to who is living the life.)

You are the mind of the spirit that God called into existence. This is what was done by the calling.

> And the Lord God formed the man of the dust of the ground, and breathed into his nostrils the breath of life: and man became a living soul. (Gen. 2:7)

The body of man was formed from the ground, and the spirit was blown into the man, and the soul was created.

> So God created man in his own image, in the image of God created he him; male and female created he them. (Gen. 1:27)

The soul is the place of the mind—the inner person. This is the answer to the question of who the mind is.

Again, you are the mind. Spiritually, we as the mind, are to become the mind of Christ.

The Bible says in 1 Corinthians 2:16 that

> For who hath know the mind of the Lord, that he may instruct him? But we have the mind of Christ.

You are to become renewed, recreated, and redeemed. You are to become the image of Christ, the renewed image of God. In the beginning God created Adam who fell, and sin came to live in every man.

For the Bible says in Romans 3:23 that

> For all have sinned, and come short of the glory of God.

What God had created in the beginning, sin had destroyed. So now we come back to God, and we are reborn back into the image of God.

> So God created man in his own image, in the image of God created he him; male and female created he them. (Gen. 1:27)

Spiritually, we are reborn back into the image of God. We become the children of God.

> The Spirit itself beareth witness with our spirit, that we are the children of God. (Rom. 8:16)

Now it is time for every man to become renewed by allowing his mind to be renewed by the Holy Ghost.

The Bible says this in Romans 12:2.:

> And be not conformed to this world: but be ye transformed by the renewing of your mind; that ye may prove what is that good, and acceptable, and perfect will of God.

Once this is done, the man becomes recreated in the image of Christ Jesus, and once man is recreated, man is redeemed and allowed back in the presence of God.

The book of Revelation 5:9 says,

> And they sung a new song, saying, Thou art worthy to take the book, and to open the seals thereof: for thou wast slain, and hast redeemed us to God by thy blood out of every kindred, and tongue, and people, and nation.

Yeah, spiritual beginning.
God has done this for us.
This is to glorify God!

A TINGLING SPIRITUAL TRINITY
THE TRINITARIAN GOD

> Herein is love, not that we loved God, but that he loved us, and sent his Son to be the propitiation for our sins.
>
> —1 John 4:10 (KJV)

I believe this to be the wisdom, knowledge, and understanding of the essence of God's love for his children—the human race. Tingling is a sensation brought through the spiritual admiration of God for his children.

It says in Romans 8:16 that

> The Spirit itself beareth witness with our spirit, that we are the children of God.

The spirituality of God's love was so great that God himself became a Father. The Bible says that we might receive the adoption of sons.

Galatians 4:6 says that

> And because ye are sons, God hath sent forth the Spirit of his Son into your hearts, crying Abba, Father.

We accept God as our Father once we accept Jesus Christ as our Lord and Savior in faith. Through his own Holy Spirit, God gave the holy seed to the woman named Mary that brought forth the body of Jesus.

> Now the birth of Jesus Christ was on this wise: When as his mother was espoused to Joseph, before they came together, she was found with child of the Holy Ghost. (Matt. 1:18, KJV)

This is how God had a Son who was the body that God walked the earth in. His name was Jesus Christ, the Son of God.

In Trinitarian terms, this meant that God was all three parts of the becoming of the Son. It was God's plan to create a door that would lead his children home, a door way back into the presence of God himself.

> Surely the righteous shall give thanks unto thy name: the upright shall dwell in thy presence. (Ps. 140:13, KJV)

God became the Father by giving the holy seed to the woman. The Spirit of God, the Holy Ghost, was the deliverer of the holy seed that was planted in the woman. The seed of God is what brought forth the child Jesus, the Son of God.

> The beginning of the gospel of Jesus Christ, the Son of God. (Mark 1:1, KJV)

It was through this holy union that all of God lived in the body of Jesus. Born as a child, Jesus had the mind of God. All the power of God was laid upon Jesus as a dove.

It states in John1:32 that

> And John bare record, saying, I saw the Spirit descending from heaven like a dove, and it abode upon him.

This happened sometime about thirty years into his life. These three parts—the Father, the Son, and the Holy Ghost—are God. They are what makes God the Trinity a union of three parts. These three parts are the images of God. The image of the Father is the image of God who loves his Son.

> And lo a voice from heaven, saying, This is my beloved Son, in whom I am well pleased. (Matt. 3:17, KJV)

The image of the Son is the image of God who walked the earth.

> And the Word was made flesh, and dwelt among us, (and we beheld his glory, the glory as of the only begotten of the Father,) full of grace and truth. (John 1:14)

And the image of the Holy Ghost is the image of God who is the Holy Spirit.

> This is he that came by water and blood, even Jesus Christ; not by water only, but by water and blood. And it is the Spirit that beareth witness, because the Spirit is truth. (1 John 5:6, KJV)

These three makes up the Trinity, the one and only Trinitarian. This means the three are one God. God is the word that God spoke into existence through the Holy Ghost, who is God's Holy Spirit, which made God a Father by bringing forth his Son—Jesus Christ. The word is the Son who came out of God through the Spirit of God that made God a Father.

John 1:1 states that

> In the beginning was the Word, and the Word was with God, and the Word was God.

The Spirit of God is true. The word was spoken into the woman, Mary, by the Holy Ghost. This created the body for God to enter of his own time. God had to come through water and blood. God had to walk in the flesh like a man. God stepped out of eternity into time to provide us with a way back into his presence. God became the door, Jesus Christ, the Creator, the Savior, and the Redeemer of his own children.

> So God created man in his own image, in the image of God created he him; male and female created he them. (Gen. 1:27, KJV)

God created man. God is the savior of men. 1 Timothy 4:10 states that

> For therefore we both labour and suffer reproach, because we trust in the living God, who is the Savior of all men, specially of those that believe.

God is the Creator of men, God is the savior of men, and God is the redeemer of men.

Isaiah 49:26 says,

> And all flesh shall know that I the Lord am thy Savior and thy Redeemer, the mighty One of Jacob.

This is the tingling spiritual Trinity—our God.

God came to deliver us from the corruption of sin and make us his children. As Jesus Christ, God created man and provided us with redemption and salvation.

This is all based on faith.

> For therein is the righteousness of God revealed from faith to faith: as it is written, the just shall live by faith. (Rom. 1:17, KJV)

For without faith, there is no pleasing God. Faith is a gift from God to those he loves.

> But without faith it is impossible to please him; for he that cometh to God must believe that he is, and that he is a rewarder of them that diligently seek him. (Heb. 11:6, KJV)

Find the time to thank the tingling spiritual Trinity who is our God, the Trinitarian, the one and only God.

Thank him for your creation, salvation, and redemption.

In the name of our Lord Jesus Christ, this is to glorify God!

ADAM, GOD'S CREATED SON, WAS NOT GOD'S BORN-AGAIN SON

> Lift up your eyes on high, and behold who hath created these things, that bringeth out their host by number: he calleth them by name by the greatness of his might, for that he is strong in power: not one faileth.
> —Isaiah 40:26

This is the Lord God, He that created the Father, the Son, and the Holy Ghost. These three are the ones that created Adam in their own image.

Adam was God's created son. To be born again takes faith in God.

This is learned.

The created son was made under the will of God (that's how he operated—doing only what God willed him to do).

> So God created man in his own image, in the image of God created he him; male and female created he them. (Gen. 1:27)

In order for the created son to become a born-again son, sin had to be placed in man. (This is the inspired revilement given from the Spirit of God. Where else would this thinking come from?)

Genesis 3:6 says that

> And when the woman saw that the tree was good for food, and that it was pleasant to the eyes, and a tree to be desired to make one wise, she took of the fruit thereof, and did eat, and gave also unto her husband with her; and he did eat.

This was God's reason for creating Lucifer with iniquity in him. Lucifer gave birth to sin in the beginning before man was created. Long before we were created, God had a plan for us. This plan was for us to become his children.

Romans 8:16 says that

> The Spirit itself beareth witness with our spirit, that we are the children of God.

I believe God knows all things, and all things are created to God's will and created according to God's plans. In the beginning was time, the beginning of the concept for man's thinking and comprehension. God himself would not put sin in man for God loved man in a way that God wanted man to share in on this love.

The Bible says that God commanded his love toward us. This is in the book of Romans 5:8 which states that

> But God commanded his love towards us, in that, while we were yet sinners, Christ died for us.

God showed his love for us by coming to earth and dying for our sins. Love must love. Love is the most powerful force of comprehension. This is why God created Lucifer, to be the flip side of love. Love only helps. Lucifer will not help for he is a liar. Lucifer is the devil, the father of lies.

The Bible calls Satan a liar in the end part of the scripture in John 8:44 which says,

> When he speaketh a lie, he speaketh of his own: for he is a liar, and the father of it.

But how could man comprehend this love of God? How could man know that this love is God, and how would man love God of his own free will?

So God had a plan to create his own children.

> That if thou shalt confess with thou mouth the Lord Jesus, and shalt believe in thine heart that God hath raised him from the dead, thou shalt be saved. (Romans 10:9, KJV)

This is the first step in becoming a child of God. God's children were created out of the love of God, in the image of God. They were born in sin, and of their own free will, chose to rid themselves of that sin by having faith. Faith to believe God's Word.

The Bible says in the book of Hebrews 11:1 that

> Now faith is the substance of things hoped for, the evidence of things not seen.

As sinners, our faith is to be saved. This is the substance hoped for, and God is the provider of the things not seen for us today. This would be Jesus Christ. God's Word is Jesus the Christ, the born-again Son of God. Through a woman named Mary, Jesus came into this world.

> Now the birth of Jesus Christ was on this wise: When as his mother Mary was espoused to Joseph, before they came together, she was found with child of the Holy Ghost. (Matt. 1:18, KJV)

The reason for the coming of Jesus was to save the world and man from sin. God allowed man to come into lowness within himself. This makes man see that he needs help and that man needs to be loved, so man calls on God.

The Bible says in Revelation 3:20 that

> Behold, I stand at the door, and knock: if any man hear my voice, and open the door, I will come in to him, and will sup with him, and he with me.

Once man realizes he needs God, the Spirit of God draws him to the truth. A truth Satan could not comprehend for God did not place it in Satan, yet God created Satan perfectly without truth.

> Thou wast perfect in thy ways from the day that thou wast created, till iniquity was found in thee. (Ezek. 28:15, kjv)

This is why Satan can't conceive the truth.

God did not allow truth in Satan. This is how sin works—it is a lie that brings about fear, and Satan is the father of lies. I believe it is through fear our attention is brought to God to ask for help. It is only God who can save man from sin. So by accepting Jesus Christ as our Savior, we come out of sin and come in to the marvelous light of God. The Bible says this in the book of 1 Peter 2:9 which states,

> But ye are a chosen generation, a royal priesthood, an holy nation, a peculiar people; that ye should shew forth the praises of him who hath called you out of darkness into his marvelous light.

As we are pulled out of darkness, we are called into the marvelous light of God.

We become born again.

We are taught to become the children of God.

This is to glorify God!

THE ANOINTED ONES

> Then said he, these are the two anointed ones, that stand by the Lord of the whole earth.
> —Zechariah 4:14 (KJV)

I pray that what I am receiving is from the Holy Spirit of God because I believe that this is telling me that the Lord Jesus Christ and the Holy Ghost are the two anointed Ones. I believe that the Lord of the whole earth is God the Father—and who else but the Son, and the Holy Spirit standing beside him?

> Be silent, O all flesh, before the Lord: for he is raised up out of his holy habitation. (Zech. 2:13, KJV)

Because God lives in me then greater is He that lives in me than he that dwells in the sin of my flesh. So I believe that this scripture is saying to me that my flesh is not to speak to our Lord. God's holy habitation is God's temple. The place where He dwells is the soul of man. God lives in the minds of men. The consciousness of man's thoughts is the Spirit that God gave us that brought them to life. The man's processing place of thinking, which is the soul, is the place where the man thinks. . The mind is his soul. This is what can't be seen, the mind or soul. We, as God's children, know that God is an unseen spiritual being, and that He has never been seen.

In the book of Romans it is proven that God is our Father.

> To all that be in Rome, beloved of God, called to be saints: Grace to you and peace from God our Father, and the Lord Jesus Christ. (Rom. 1:7, KJV)

This scripture proves that God is our Father, the provider of the life of men.

In the book of Hebrews 1:8 the Bible proves that the Son is God.

> But unto the Son he saith, Thy throne, O God, is forever and ever: a scepter of righteousness is the scepter of thy kingdom.

Here the Son is called God.

In Acts 5:3–4, Ananias lied to the Holy Ghost, a trick of Satan's. In reality he didn't lie to man but to God.

This is what verse 4 says.

This is clearly expressing that the Holy Ghost is God.

> But Peter said, "Ananias, why hath Satan filled thine heart to lie to the Holy Ghost, and to keep back part of the price of the land? Whiles it remained, was it not thine own? Why hast thou conceived this thing in thine heart? Thou hast not lied unto man, but unto God." (Acts 5:3–4, KJV)

And again this scripture proves that the Holy Ghost is God. The Father, the Son, and the Holy Ghost—all three are God. These Three are the images God revealed himself as, God the Father, the Son and the Holy Ghost.

So as it was mentioned, the two anointed ones, I believe, are Jesus Christ and the Holy Ghost.

This is to glorify God!

Amen!

BEFORE I BECAME FLESH, I WAS THE CREATED IMAGE OF GOD GUIDED BY THE WILL OF GOD!

> So God created man in his own image, in the image of God created he him; male and female created he them.
>
> —Genesis 1:27 (KJV)

In God's beginning of man, God created man in his own image. We look like the shining light of God with splendor but no life. Life came to man when God gave man his Spirit.

> And the Lord God formed man of the dust of the ground, and breathed into his nostrils the breath of life; and man became a living soul. (Gen. 2:7)

The image of God is the soul, because it thinks. This is the image of God I see in my mind. I see this because of my own soul, and I am the created image of God. The image of God is a spirit because that is what he is—a Spirit with a soul that thinks, a spiritual being full of life, full of holiness, and full of love.

> Behold, what manner of love the Father hath bestowed upon us, that we should be called the sons of God: therefore the world knoweth us not, because it knew him not. (1 John 3:1, KJV)

The image of God appears in the flesh because He wanted us to know him exclusively, and for us to know him of our own free will.

The Bible speaks of this in John 1:14 which states,

> And the Word was made flesh, and dwelt among us, (and we beheld his glory, the glory as of the only begotten of the Father,) full of grace and truth.

The soul and spirit can not be physically seen. The Bible reveals that God was formed and made flesh in Isaiah 43:10.

> Ye are my witnesses, saith the Lord, and my servant whom I have chosen; that ye may know and believe me, and understand that I am he: before me there was no God formed, neither shall there be after me.

This soul was the image of God—something that we were once made out of before we became flesh. The soul defines who we are, and the Spirit is what gives us life. God gave us life by giving us his Spirit, which was his breath of life.

The Bible reveals that Jesus explains God as a Spirit in John 4:24 which states,

> God is a Spirit: and they that worship him must worship him in spirit and in truth.

The truth here is that God is Spirit. This is why our life belongs to God. Our life is the Spirit of God, given to us through the nostrils of flesh by God. God blew the spirit in man and made man a living soul.

Without the Spirit, our soul would be lifeless.

We are that we are because we think.

We think because we have life.

Our life is a gift of God given as his Spirit.

> God that made the world and all things therein, seeing that he is Lord of heaven and earth, dwelleth not in temples made with hands. (Acts 17:24, KJV)

As long as God's Spirit lives in us, we shall live according to the will of God.

> I am crucified with Christ: nevertheless I live; yet not I, but Christ liveth in me: and the life which I now live in the flesh I live by the faith of the Son of God, who loved me, and gave himself for me. (Gal. 2:20, KJV)

Now that I know that I am a soul with the life of God in me, I plan to live according to God's will. It is his life that I am alive in. It is his Spirit that is in me, that is what makes me in him. God is our God, and we are his children.

It is the Spirit that reveals this to us.

> The Spirit itself beareth witness with our spirit, that we are the children of God. (Rom. 8:16, KJV)

Our faith in the Lord Jesus Christ is what makes us the children of God. It is by our faith that we are what God wants us to become . Christ is the power of God whose will is what guides our life and is according to God's will for our life in the name of our Lord Jesus Christ.

> But we all, with open face beholding as in a glass the glory of the Lord, are changed into the same image from glory to glory, even as by the Spirit of the Lord. (2 Cor. 3:18, KJV)

Our Lord is the Spirit who is changing us into his image and glory. It is God's image we all are created in.

God makes us all holy through redemption.

This is to glorify God!

BELIEF, BELIEVE, AND THE BELIEVER
BY FAITH IN JESUS CHRIST

> And such were some of you: but ye are washed, but ye are sanctified, but ye are justified in the name of the Lord Jesus, and by the Spirit of our God.
> —1 Corinthians 6:11 (KJV)

Belief, taught to us by the Father, for the looking toward faith.

> Therefore being justified by faith, we have peace with God through our Lord Jesus Christ. (Rom. 5:1, KJV)

Wherefore the law was our schoolmaster to bring us unto Christ, that we might be justified by faith.

The believer is being that person of faith, in Jesus Christ. The Bible's belief is the true fact that if we believe in the Lord Jesus Christ, the Holy Ghost will transform us to be like Christ, a true believer in our God.

This is to glorify God!

CONSCIOUS LIFE

> Let this mind be in you, which was also in Christ Jesus.
> —Philippians 2:5

Christ is all the power of God that lived in Jesus, and Jesus is he who had the mind of God. I received a thought that God is the mind that thinks within the soul of his Spirit. A thought is conscious life—life that's being lived within the soul of the Spirit of God. This conscious life is an unseen power of thought that lives. There is the Spirit, within the Spirit is the soul, and within the soul is the mind. This is the mind of Christ who is all of the power of God.

> But unto them which are called, both Jews and Greeks, Christ the power of God, and the wisdom of God. (1 Cor. 1:24, KJV)

The mind would be of the Father, the soul would be of the Son, and the Spirit would be of the Holy Ghost. The Three are one—God. The Bible verifies this in the book of 1 John 5:7 which says,

> For there are three that bear record in heaven, the Father, the Word, and the Holy Ghost: and these three are one.

The soul within the spirit is alive because it has a mind that thinks.

The Bible shows us that we have the mind of Christ.

> For who hath known the mind of the Lord, that he may instruct him? But we have the mind of Christ. (1 Cor. 2:16)

Thinking is done by the life that is the consciousness. To be conscious, one must be alive. It is the mind of God—Christ—that is alive.

The Bible reveals this in the book of Revelation 1:18 which says,

> I am he that liveth, and was dead; and, behold, I am alive for evermore, Amen; and have the keys of hell and of death.

There has been, there is, and there will always be a conscious life—the mind of Christ who is God. Conscious life is the essence of God. It is the invisible and unseen power of God who is alive.

This is to glorify God!

CREATED WITHOUT SIN, ADAM?

> And God said, Let us make man in our image, after our likeness: and let them have dominion over the fish of the sea, and over the fowl of the air, and over the cattle, and over all the earth, and over ever creeping thing that creepeth upon the earth.
> —Genesis 1:26 (KJV)

Adam was created with the righteousness, the goodness, and the truth of God. There was no sin in him. Adam is, was, and will always be created in the very likeness of God. Adam was created to operate in the likeness of God's will. Meaning, he lived according to what God willed. What God willed was God's own image, the likeness of God's own self—Love (for God is Love).

The Bible says this about the love of God in Romans 8:38–39,

> For I am persuaded, that neither death, nor life, nor angels, nor principalities, nor powers, nor things present, nor things to come, Nor height, nor depth, nor any other

> creature, shall be able to separate us from the love of God, which is in Christ Jesus our Lord.

Adam was created to operate under God's will. God gave Adam his own will, but there was no reason for Adam to use it. Adam lived under, in, and through God. Adam had the mind of God.

> Let this mind be in you, which was also in Christ Jesus. (Phil. 2:5)

What was in Christ was the mind of God that which was in Adam. There was no reason for Adam to think outside of God for he thought as God thought. We step in front of a mirror and see our image. We create the image in the mirror by stepping in to the front of it. If we do not step in front of the mirror, there is no image. Everything we see in the mirror is the image of self.

Adam was the created image of God. God revealed himself to Adam as Adam's Creator by allowing Adam to name all the animals—this was how Adam knew that God was God, and that he was God's created son.

> And out of the ground the Lord God formed every beast of the field, and every fowl of the air; and brought them unto Adam to see what he would call them: and whatsoever

> Adam called every living creature, that was
> the name thereof. (Gen. 2:19)

God reveals that the two spirits were one because Adam's spirit had the same conceptual image of God's mind. They walked, talked, and thought alike. Adam knew that he was the created son and that he was not born of God. Adam also knew that God had a plan that would make him a born-again son. The mind of God was revealed to Adam (that he would have the complete comprehension of being born again), the moment God created him a woman—Eve. Once Eve was created, Adam would know what God was planning. So as God put Adam to sleep and removed one of his ribs.

The Bible depicts this in Genesis 2:21 which says,

> And the Lord God caused a deep sleep to
> fall upon Adam, and he slept: and he took
> one of his ribs, and closed up the flesh
> instead thereof.

God formed Eve from one of Adam's ribs.

> And the rib, which the Lord God had
> taken from the man, made he a woman, and
> brought her unto the man. (Gen. 2:22)

The woman was formed from the rib of man by God. Adam was formed from the dust of the ground by God.

This is a God-given revealment from the Spirit of the Lord. Eve was birthed or formed out of Adam, and they were one. My spirit is complacent.

This is why Adam said Eve was bone of his bone and flesh of his flesh.

> And Adam said, This is now bone of my bones, and flesh of my flesh: she shall be called Woman, because she was taken out of Man. (Gen. 2:2)

The woman and the man are capital because they are the created image of God—without sin. Eve was formed from Adam, and Eve was taught by Adam the things of God. Adam operated under the will of God; he did what God willed for his life. Adam thought according to the will of God, until Eve was deceived.

> And when the woman saw that the tree was good for food, and that it was pleasant to the eyes, and a tree to be desired to make one wise, she took of the fruit thereof, and did eat, and gave also unto her husband with her; and he did eat. (Gen. 3:6, KJV)

This was the (First) time Adam used his own free will. Adam used it because he knew this was the main reason why God had given it to him, to walk in, to walk through, and to walk out of sin by faith. This way Adam would comprehend the fullness of God and become born again. Only by experiencing sin could Adam ever be born of God. Without sin, there was no need to be born again, no need to be saved. No way for Adam to become a born-of-God child. No way for Adam to know the fullness of God.

Sin had to come.

This is how we learn the fullness of God's love for us. It is through Adam that we all are born in sin. Remember Lucifer fell, and the sin fell with him. God threw him down to the pit of hell in Earth.

> How art thou fallen from heaven, O Lucifer, son of the morning! how art thou cut down to the ground, which didst weaken the nations! (Isa. 14:12)

Sin was in the world because Lucifer was here, and where there is Lucifer, there is sin. This sin was in Lucifer before man was created, and Lucifer was in the world before man. It was Lucifer (Satan) that placed sin in man. Lucifer defiled the world just as well as Lucifer defiled man. (Sin was placed in them both from the beginning of the time of man.) This is what God allowed so that we would walk into sin, that we would walk through sin, and by faith, walk out of sin.

> Now we have received, not the spirit of the world, but the spirit which is of God; that

> we might know the things that are freely
> given to us of God. (1 Cor. 2:12, KJV)

The Father walked with us into sin, Jesus Christ walked through sin with us, and the Holy Ghost, through faith, walked us out of sin. Adam was created without sin. Adam was the likeness of God. Adam had the mind of God. There was no other likeness (but God) for Adam to follow after. There was no other image for Adam to emulate but God. What Adam understood about being born again was what the Bible talks about in 1 Peter 1:23 (KJV) which says,

> Being born again, not of corruptible seed, but of incorruptible, by the word of God, which liveth and abideth for ever.

This is to glorify God!

CREATOR, REDEEMER, AND REVEALER
GOD IS JESUS CHRIST

> That was the true Light, which lighteth every man that cometh into the world.
> —John 1:9

Every man that comes into the world is created by God. Every man who sins is brought back to God and freed of sin by Jesus Christ. This is Jesus Christ, the Creator. The Redeemer is revealed to be God in the book of Psalms 78:35 which says,

> And they remembered that God was their rock, and the high God their redeemer.

A redeemer is a person who intervenes and pays a necessary price to win the release of another from some bondage or danger. This is according to the *Revell Bible Dictionary*.

The Bible reveals within itself a scriptural definition in 1 Corinthians 2:10 which says,

> But God hath revealed them unto us by his
> Spirit: for the Spirit searcheth all things,
> yea, the deep things of God.

This is what Jesus Christ has done for us all—he has freed us from the bondage and danger of sin. We already have the victory. It is our job to walk by faith in the will of God, according to the spiritual promises of God. The Bible tells us that we receive the Spirit of God so we can know the things of God.

> Now we have received, not the spirit of the
> world, but the spirit which is of God; that
> we might know the things that are freely
> given to us of God. (1 Cor. 2:12)

God, the Revealer, is revealed in Daniel 2:47 which says,

> The king answered unto Daniel, and said,
> Of a truth it is, that your God is a God of
> gods, and a Lord of kings, and a revealer
> of secrets, seeing thou couldest reveal this
> secret.

God is our Creator, our Redeemer and our Revealer. God is Jesus Christ.

The Bible unveils this in the book of 1 John 5:20 which says,

> And we know that the Son of God is come, and hath given us understanding, that we may know him that is true, and we are in him that is true, even in his Son Jesus Christ. This is the true God, and eternal life.

Jesus Christ is God the Creator, the Redeemer, and the Revealer.

This is to glorify God!

FAITH IS THE BODY OF HOLINESS

> So then faith cometh by hearing, and hearing by the word of God.
> —Romans 10:17, KJV

This is the Word of God the Father, and faith comes from the Father. The body is the Son.

> There is one body, and one Spirit, even as ye are called in one hope of your calling. (Ephesians 4:4, KJV)

This body is the Lord Jesus Christ. Christ Jesus is the hope of our calling. God calls the believers to become his adopted children—renewed men.

> And that ye put on the new man, which after God is created in righteousness and true holiness. (Eph. 4:24)

This holiness is of the Holy Ghost, the one who bears witness in heaven. The Bible says in 1 John 5:7 (KJV) that

> For there are three that bear record in heaven, the Father, the Word, and the Holy Ghost: and that theses three are one.

These three are of one spirit—the Spirit of God. We, the believers, are born of God and delivered through faith by the body of holiness. This body is that of the Son of God.

> And I saw, and bare record that this is the Son of God. (John 1:34, KJV)

We are delivered through faith in Christ Jesus by the Spirit of God, the Holy Ghost. The Holy Ghost is he who gives birth to the children of God. That means he transforms our old ways to new ways. The Bible says that we are to be transformed.

> And be not conformed to this world: but be ye transformed by the renewing of your mind, that ye may prove what is that good, and acceptable, and perfect, will of God. (Rom. 12:2, KJV)

Our faith is planted in Christ Jesus like seeds of men planted in a woman, and the Holy Ghost becomes pregnant, meaning transformational. Then the Holy Ghost transforms our faith in Christ Jesus so that we are to become like Jesus Christ. The Holy Ghost gives birth or transforms our renewed soul and renewed spirit. This is the transformation as being born again.

> Jesus answered and said unto him, Verily, verily I say unto thee, Except a man be born again, he cannot see the kingdom of God. (John 3:3, KJV)

Being born again is when you come out of corruptible sin and live in the incorruptible righteousness of God.

You who have an ear for the Spirit.

May you hear what the Spirit of God has to reveal. Our spirit is taught, trained, and guided by the Holy Ghost.

> For the Holy Ghost shall teach you in the same hour what you ought to say. (Luke 12:12, KJV)

Our spirit then teaches our soul the will of God for our lives. Our spirit then teaches our souls to become the children of God.

> The Spirit itself beareth witness with our spirit, that we are the children of God. (Rom. 8:16, KJV)

Our spirit is given to us by God. Our faith is given to us by God the Father. It is by the body of the Son of God, who shed his blood and died at Calvary, that our faith comes from and lives in. This holiness is of the Holy Ghost, who is the spirit of God. The body of holiness is physically seen as the Lord Jesus Christ. As we give our lives to Christ, our faith lives in him.

Amen!

Faith is the body of holiness!

This is to glorify God!

FROM A SEED TO A TREE

> The Lord God placed the man in the
> Garden of Eden to tend and care for it.
> —Genesis 2:15 (NLT)

Martha P. Brown is my garden of Eden. She is the birthplace where I, as a seed, lived my life under the will of God. God placed me within my mother from the beginning when His way began, even before the creation of the world.

> The Lord already possessed "Me" long ago, when His way began, before any of His works. (Prov. 8:22)

It is here in the womb—our place of genesis, our beginning, and our Eden—that our wisdom is accessible only to our Creator.

> You made all of the delicate, inner parts of my body and knit "Me" together in my mother's womb. (Ps. 139:13, NLT)

Here in Eden, the master of wisdom, God, feeds us the spiritual understandings—the priorities for life. The Holy Spirit has instilled in us the Word of God.

> I will put my laws in their minds and I will write them on their hearts. (Jer. 31:33)

The priority for life is the Word of God. Every mother feeds their children with the right amount of nourishment. The Word of God is like the milk that a baby drinks in order to be filled. The Bible says that God put his Word in us. The Word is the Lord Jesus Christ.

> In the beginning was the Word, and the Word was with God, and the Word was God. (John 1:1)

This is how we are changed from a seed to a tree. While we were in a seedlike state of existence, living our lives without Christ, we were not yet what God's Spirit willed us to become. As a seed, we needed to be planted in good spiritual ground.

We need to be mentally aware of our spiritual nature and be deeply rooted in the study of God's Word. Studying and reading God's Word will help us, as seeds, to grow.

The Father will teach us his values. It is through our faith in the Son of God that our thoughts are trained in the wisdom, knowledge, and understanding of God. It is the Holy Spirit who guides, educates, and develops our spirit. He transforms us, our seedlike existence, to be like Christ. Under his guidance, we can become trees full of God's wisdom, knowledge, and understanding.

Along with His guidance comes insight and foresight pertaining to the things of God. A seed must first die and then be planted in the soil to become a tree.

> You fool! The seed you plant doesn't come to life unless it dies first. What you plant, whether its wheat or something else, is only a seed. It doesn't have the form that the plant will have. God gives the plant the form he wants it to have. Each kind of seed grows into its own form. (1 Cor. 15:36–38)

We must surrender our lives to God by accepting Jesus Christ as our Lord and Savior. In doing this, the selfish ruling of our own lives will come to an end, and we allow God to rule our lives. The moment we do this, we are given life in Him. Christ comes to live in us.

> For in him we live, and move, and have our being; as certain also of your own poets have said, "For we are also his offspring." (Acts 17:28, KJV)

As Christ died and was risen, our seed died and began to blossom. God wants all of us to be saved. He wants to recreate us to be like Christ.

> For God know his people in advance, and he chose them to become like his Son; so that his Son would be the firstborn, with many brothers and sisters. (Rom 8:29, NLT)

We are created beings—seeds—who God has called to become his children.

> The first man, Adam, became a living person. But the last Adam-that is, Christ-is a life giving spirit. What came first was the natural body, and then the spiritual body comes later. Adam, the first man, was made from the dust of the earth, while, the second man, came from heaven. Every human being has an earthly body just like Adam's, but our heavenly bodies will be just like Christ's. Just as we are now like Adam, the man of the earth, so we will someday be like Christ, the man from heaven. (1 Cor. 15:45–49, NLT)

Just as the seed is planted in the earth, must our bodies also be planted in the ground?

The seed is resurrected and given new life as a tree. In the same way shall our bodies be lifted up as heavenly bodies in the image of Christ. So we, *the seed*, become the tree, *the image of Christ*.

1. *We* are created in the image of The Father.
2. The *tree* represents the image of the Son we were destined to be like.
3. The Holy Spirit is the power by which we are transformed (to be like Christ).

We, the tree, are the transformed into the image of Christ.

While here on earth, we walk in the flesh by faith in the promises of God.

This is to glorify God

Amen!

GOD CREATED SATAN, SATAN CREATED SIN, GOD CREATED US

> Thou art the anointed cherub that covereth; and I have set thee so: thou wast upon the holy mountain of God; thou hast walked up and down in the midst of the stones of fire.
> —Ezekiel 28:14 (kjv)

God created Satan with the wisdom, the knowledge, and the understanding that out of Satan would come iniquity.

God knows everything—past, present, and future.

> Thou wast perfect in thy ways from the day that thou wast created, till iniquity was found in thee. (Ezek. 28:15, kjv)

These are God words—*thou wast created*.
God created Satan, Satan created iniquity.
What caused Satan to create sin?

> Thine heart was lifted up because of thy beauty, thou hast corrupted thy wisdom by reason of thy brightness: I will cast thee to the ground, I will lay thee before kings, that they may behold thee. (Ezek. 28:17, KJV)

God created Satan full of beauty. Because of this beauty, pride developed in Satan, and Satan proclaimed himself to be God's equal.

> Therefore thus saith the Lord God; Because thou hast set thine heart as the heart of God. (Ezek. 28:6)

This was the iniquity that was found in Satan. This was *sin*.

> By the multitude of thy merchandise they have filled the midst of thee with violence, and thou hast sinned: therefore I will cast thee as profane out of the mountain of God: and I will destroy the, O covering cherub, from the midst of the stones of fire. (Ezek. 28:16)

Satan chose to have his heart set as the heart of God and in doing so, brought out sin. This sin was in Satan, and Satan was in the world before man was created. God kicked Satan out of heaven before God created man. The iniquity found in Satan was sin. God threw him down to the lower parts of the earth with sin in him.

> How are thou fallen from heaven, O Lucifer, son of the morning! How art thou cut down to the ground, which didst weaken the nations? Yet thou shalt be brought down to hell, to the sides of the pit. (Isa. 14:12, 15, KJV)

I believe Satan was a spiritual being, so the sin in him would be unseen by the eyes of a man. This is how Satan was cleverly able to put sin in man (this was not until after God had created man).

Yes, God created man.

> So God created man in his own image, in the image of God created he him; male and female created he them. (Gen. 1:27, KJV)

God created us for his plan. As I said, sin was in the world. God created us to learn the difference between God and Satan. We are to learn that the better of the two is love (God). Sin is of the devil, and love is of God. The chooser is us.

We are the point in the middle.

The horizon is Jesus Christ, the line between God and Satan.

We, as the chooser, should choose of our own free will to look toward the Horizon, Jesus Christ. God created us to become the children of God.

> For ye are all the Children of God by faith in Christ Jesus. (Gal. 3:26, KJV)

The Son of God is clearly the divide between God and Satan. This is why God created us. God wants us to become like Christ. He wants us to become his child. In order to be a child of God, we must learn to set sin aside and walk by faith in the Word of God.

> For we walk by faith, not by sight. (2 Cor. 5:7, KJV)

This sin would be used as the major part of God's plan to teach us God's will for our lives. Satan's spiritual sin would be the tool that would be used to teach us about the love of God.

> For this is the love of God, that we keep his commandments: and his commandments are not grievous. (1 John 5:3, KJV)

Satan is Lucifer, the devil. He has the power to transform himself.

> And no marvel; for Satan himself is transformed into an angel of light. (2 Cor. 11:14, kjv)

Lucifer was the cherub, the angel that God created in the beginning. God found iniquity in Lucifer (this was the created sin), and then God created man.

Like Jesus we are in the middle of the promises of God.

The promise of God is eternal life.

> For the wages of sin is death; but the gift of God is eternal life through Jesus Christ our Lord. (Rom. 6:23, kjv)

God offers eternal life to us if we believe with faith in his Son. We either believe God, or we believe the lies of Satan. God created us to be wise. We are to look to the Horizon, to the power of God. This is a must if we are to be saved, and we are to choose Jesus Christ who is the horizon between God and the devil.

God, the devil, and man.

The Spirit reveals that God uses the devil to teach man the true power of love. Because of sin, man learns to stay away from the devil, by setting sin aside. This is done through Jesus Christ our Lord. It is our faith, our trust, and our belief in Jesus Christ that Christ has used for our souls to be redeemed. Our faith in the Father, our trust in the Son and our belief in the Holy Ghost are all a gift of

God that we are to learn in this walk of life. God, Satan, and us—there is only the horizon for us to look forward to. It is He who will help us make the right choices, and He is the Lord Jesus the Christ, the Lord Jesus Christ. God created Satan as a spiritually anointed cherub, an angel that would give birth to sin. God would use this sin to bring God's created man into becoming born again. The King James Version of John 3:7 states, "Marvel not that I said unto thee, ye must be born again." This is an act of us, the believers, that we are to become born of God. This is what makes man a child of God. This was God's plan when God's way began. In the God's Word, Today's Translation of Proverbs 8:22, it says that, "The Lord already possessed me long ago, when his way began, before any of his works." This is the wisdom of God, which is Christ, the Word of God. In the Bible, John 1:1 states that, "In the beginning was the Word, and the Word was with God, and the Word was God." God is, was, and will always be a spiritual being of love. God cares for us.

This is to glorify God!

GOD HAS A TIME AND DATE FOR ALL OF US

> Remember the former things of old: for I am God, and there is none else: I am God, and there is none like me.
> —Isaiah 46:9 (KJV)

Our times and dates are set according to God's will. There is a time to live and there is a time to die—both set by God's will. It is God's will for us to live a fruitful life, a life helping others to come to Christ to be saved.

> Look unto me, and be ye saved, all the ends of the earth: for I am God, and there is none else. (Isa. 45:22, KJV)

God has given us life to become saved and to become his children. We are meant to shine or reflect God's glory to the world. We are vessels planted here on earth to die and to become born again of God's Spirit, meaning we are to, of our own free will, give our life to Christ through faith. We must learn to trust Christ. We must believe that the blood of Christ will cover us and that Christ died on the cross to redeem, forgive, and save us. This is God's will for our life—redemption, forgiveness, and salvation. God wants us to become delivered, baptized, and holy beings, and he wants us back in his presence.

> Tell ye, and bring them near; yea, let them take counsel together: who hath declared this from ancient times? Who hath told it from that time? Have not I the Lord? And there is no God else beside me; a just God and a Saviour; there is none beside me. (Isa. 45:21, KJV)

These are the words that God speaks to us according to his will. This is the time God has given us to live, learn, and love according to his will for our lives. You must believe that God is. God is the one who has given us a death date.

> Consider and hear me, O Lord my God: lighten mine eyes, lest I sleep the sleep of death. (Ps. 13:3, KJV)

This is a date in time given to all of us from God. No one knows his own date of death, only God does. If you are spiritually secure and have faith in Jesus Christ, this would be a homecoming well waited for. As it is a date the saved, the believer, long for. Now until then, may God's will guide, protect, and govern your life. For death is the doorway to heaven or hell. We, the children of God, are concerned with heaven, the place of God. We are concerned with God's love for us and the love we have for him.

> Therefore thou shalt love the Lord thy God, and keep his charge, and his statutes, and his judgments, and his commandments, always. (Deut. 1:1, KJV)

These are the concerns the renewed man's mind should be about. The renewed man is the man that is transformed by the Holy Ghost. This man has become a new creation, a man conformed to do the will of God. A man transformed to be like Christ. This is the man who died to the will of his own and became the man who does the will of God.

There is a time to live and a date to die.

All provided by the will of God for the lives he predestined for us.

> God having provided some better thing for us, that they without us should not be made perfect. (Heb. 11:40, KJV)

This means that we can't be the Christ that we are to become like until God has finished all his work within us. All of God's promises in life and in death are not received in this world. We must die to the sins of our will and be reborn of God (somewhat like Christ). God has provided us the time to live and choose, of our own free will, Jesus Christ as our Savior. With faith, our choice is Christ. We choose to die to our own will and live according to the will of God. This death causes us to live forever spiritually in the will of God.

> Not with eye service, as men pleasers; but as the servants of Christ, doing the will of God from the heart. (Eph. 6:6, KJV)

This death closes our eyes to pleasing men and causes us to become servants, the children of God. We are pleased to do the will of God because God's will now dominate our life. The Spirit of God, the Holy Ghost, has transformed us according to the will of God to become like Christ, a child of God.

> And be not conformed to this world: but be ye transformed by the renewing of your mind that ye may prove what is that good, and acceptable, and perfect, will of God. (Rom.12:2, KJV)

This is to glorify God
Amen!

GOD, THE GOOD AND GREAT FARMER

> The Spirit itself beareth witness with our spirit, that we are the children of God.
> —Romans 8:16 (KJV)

Men, the seeds of God, created in the image of God himself, were planted here on earth to become what God planned for them to become—the children of God.

> All creation is eagerly waiting for God to reveal who his children are. (Rom. 8:19, GW)

All of creation has been waiting to see the children of God. The angels asked why God cares so much for man.

> Instead, someone has declared this somewhere in scripture: What is a mortal that you should remember him, or the Son of Man that you take care of him? (Heb. 2:6, GW)

I believe it is because God is love. The very nature of love is to love. I believe God created us to be loved and cared for. Not that God needed to, but because of his nature, full of grace and mercy, God chose to give his love to the human race.

> The mystery that gives us our reverence for God is acknowledged to be great: He appeared in his human nature, was approved by the Spirit, was seen by angels, was announced throughout the nations, was believed in the world, and was taken to heaven in glory. (1 Tim. 3:16, GW)

It is in the will of God to love and care for his children.

> I will praise thee; for I am fearfully and wonderfully made. (Ps. 136:14, KJV)

We are wonderfully made by the loving hands of God in the loving image of God Himself. We were created perfect in the beginning according to the will of God.

> That the man of God may be perfect, thoroughly furnished unto all good works. (2 Tim. 3:17, KJV)

God had a plan for the man he created. This plan would allow man to become not just a created man, but an adopted born-again man.

> Being born again, not of corruptible seed, but of incorruptible, by the word of God, which liveth and abideth for ever. (1 Pet. 1:23, KJV)

In order for man to become born again, God allowed Lucifer, the devil/Satan, to place sin in man so that man would have to learn the difference between right and wrong and the difference between God and Satan. God commanded man not to eat of the tree of the knowledge of good and evil.

> And when the woman saw that the tree was good for food, and that it was pleasant to the eyes, and a tree to be desired to make one wise, she took of the fruit thereof, and did eat, and gave also unto her husband with her; and he did eat. (Gen. 2:6, KJV)

In the plan of God by the appointed time of God, man had to, choose with faith, the Lord Jesus Christ.

> Till we are all come in the unity of the faith, and of the knowledge of the Son of God, unto a perfect man, unto the measure of the stature of the fullness of Christ. (Eph. 4:13, KJV)

In doing so, man would become born again. Man would be adopted by God. The acceptance by man of the Lord Jesus Christ would allow man back in the presence of God after man fell into sin. The blood of Christ would cover all of man's sins, past, present, and future. God would accept man faultless and blameless, and forgive man for all his sins—yesterday, today, and the tomorrows to come.

> But if we walk in the light, as he is in the light, we have fellowship one with another, and the blood of Jesus Christ his Son cleanseth us from all sin. (1 John 1:7, KJV)

This is why God loved the world so much and planted man here on planet Earth. God had planned and planted man here on Earth so that man would learn, through faith, to accept Christ, and grow in the Word of God, and become like Christ. God sees man as a seed covered by the blood of Christ. God, the good and great Farmer, is the Father, Son, and Holy Ghost.

> Ye are of God, little children, and have overcome them: because greater is he that is in you, than he that is in the world. (1 John 4:4, KJV)

Amen
This is to glorify God!

GOD TRUST US

> If you know that Christ has God's approval,
> you also know that everyone who does what
> God approves of has been born from God.
> —1 John 2:29

God trust us more than we trust ourselves. This is why God trust us. When by faith, we accept Jesus as our Lord and Savior, we are born from God. God knows everything about us. He knows our present, past, and future. He knows what we think.

> The father has given us his love. He loves
> us so much that we are actually called God's
> dear children. And that's what we are. For this
> reason the world doesn't recognize us, and it
> didn't recognize him either. (1 John 3:1)

We, on the other hand, don't really know who we are. To understand the *who* in us, we must first understand the *why* we are. Meaning, why are we even who we are. We are, because God called us.

> However, if my people, who are called by my name, will humble themselves, pray, search for me, and turn from their evil ways, then I will hear their prayer from heaven, forgive their sins, and heal their county. (2 Chr. 7:14)

We had nothing to do with us being called or created. The answer to the *why we are* is God called us. The reason God called us is because of His mercy and grace, which is in His nature. This is why He created us as human beings.

> So God created humans in his image. In the image of God he created them. He created them male and female. (Gen. 1:27)

> Then the Lord God formed the man from the dust of the earth and blew the breath of life into his nostrils. The man became a living being. (Gen. 2:7)

This is the connection to the *Who* in whom we are. We are who we are because of God's love for us. His love makes us who we are. God created us to be loved by Him according to his mercy and grace.

> Do not remember the sins of my youth or my rebellious ways. Remember me O

> Lord, in keeping with your mercy and your goodness. (Ps. 25:7)

We are to be holy in the sight of God. Who we are is the creation from the notion of God's thoughts of love. Our *who* is the created image of God. This image—our likeness—is of God's image.

Who, meaning us, is like the image of God?

Now you know *the we are*, so the *who we are* is simple.

We are the created image of God. This is one reason why God knows and trust us so well. We were created to mirror God's image. The characteristic that make up who God is. God is a threefold being. God is, God was, and God will always be love.

> This is the message we heard from Christ and are reporting to you: God is light and there isn't any darkness in him. (1 John 1:5)

God is gracious, magnificent, and dignified. He is a merciful being. We were created to glorify God for his greatness, his power of creation, and his great love of us. We are God's children. God's own spirit guides us according to God's will for our lives. This Holy Spirit is the spirit of truth. This is why God can trust us because his spirit lives in us.

> However, there is in humans a Spirit, the breath of the almighty, that gives them understanding. (Job 32:8)

It is not because of anything we did that God chose to love us. God had already called us. God chose us before the creation of the world. His spirit lives within us. This is why we, as his children, know his voice.

> On earth we have fathers who discipline us, and we respect them. Shouldn't we place ourselves under the authority of God, the father of spirits, so that we will live? (Heb. 12:9)

His voice is heard deep down within us. Within our minds and hearts, God called us to come out of the darkness of this world. He called us to come back to him and to come live in our spiritual existence with Him. We were created to live in this world only for a little while, long enough to choose, of our own free will, to come back home to God, back to eternity.

We are here to learn about sin and to understand that sin is wrong. We are to reject sin and choose God. Because God is love, and sin is hate. Sin is the opposite of everything God represents. We should know now that we must choose, and that the right choice is to go home to God. All of God's children know His voice.

> The Lord thundered from the heaven. The Most High made his voice heard. (2 Sam. 22:14)

Listen with your hearts spiritual ear, and you will hear the sound of God's voice in you, calling you to come home. Come through the door who is the Lord Jesus Christ. You can only enter with faith. This is the key that opens the door. The sound of faith in motion is God's voice. It makes us who we are. God trust his voice that lives in each of us.

This is to glorify God.

Amen!

GOD'S PLAN

> The Lord of Armies has taken an oath: It will happen exactly as I've intended. It will turn out exactly as I've planned. I'll crush Assyria on my land. I'll trample it underfoot on my mountains. Then its yoke will be removed from my people, and its burden will be removed from their shoulders. This is the plan determined for the whole earth. This is how he will use his power against all the nations. The Lord of Armies has planned it. Who can stop it? He is ready to use his power. Who can turn it back?
> —Isaiah 14:24–27 (GW)

The world is in sin, but God has a plan to save it.

Here, I believe the Lord is revealing through divine intervention the fact that the Lord Jesus Christ is coming to save the world.

Jesus says in John 12:47 (GW), "If anyone hears my words and doesn't follow them, I don't condemn them. I didn't come to condemn the world but to save the world."

The Spirit reveals that Jesus Christ is going to crush Satan in his lands and trample him under Jesus's feet. Christ will take Satan's corrupt nature from the spirit of God's people. This will allow our souls to be guided, trained, and kept by the Holy Ghost—the true Spirit of God.

> And be not conformed to this world: but be ye transformed by the renewing of your mind, that ye may prove what is that good, and acceptable, and perfect, will of God. (Rom. 12:2, GW)

We are not to place the things of the world as more important than our God. There is nothing more than God. God is the Creator of all, seen and unseen. God is the Beginning and the End of all there is. God is, was, and will always be the one and only true Spiritual Being. Within God's plan, God became one of us.

> God saved us and called us to be holy, not because of what we had done, but because of his own plan and kindness. Before the world began, God planned that Christ Jesus would show us God's kindness. (2 Tim. 1:9, GW)

Before the beginning of the world, God had already planned to show us that he chose to save and make us holy. Before God created the earth, he had planned to teach us to become his children. This is why the world was created, why God loved the world so much. The world was meant to be the day care center, the garden of Eden, the place were God would plant his created beings. Here we were meant to become the children of God. We were meant to be used by Satan and sin first, then find and accept Jesus Christ and with faith and trust and believe that God raised Christ from the grave. Then let go of our will, and with faith, allow God's will to save us.

> However, when God our Savior made his kindness and love for humanity appear, he saved us, but not because of anything we had done to gain his approval. Instead, because of his mercy he saved us through the washing in which the Holy Spirit gives us new birth and renewal. God poured a generous amount of the Spirit on us through Jesus Christ our Savior. As a result, God in his kindness has given us his approval and we have become heirs who have the confidence that we have everlasting life. (Titus 3:4–7, GW)

This was done according to God's plan before the world began. Our Savior, Jesus Christ, is God's plan to save the world.

> He is the payment for our sins, and not only for our sins, but also for the sins of the whole world. (1 John 2:2, GW)

When the blood of Christ was shed on the cross at Calvary, the place of the skull, our sins and the sins of the world—pass, present, and future—were forgiven of us, the saved.

> They came to a place called Golgotha (which means "the place of the skull"). (Matt. 27:33, GW)

This is the place where Christ shed his blood for us, the sinners. The Bible verifies this in John 19:17 (GW) which states that

> He carried his own cross and went out of the city to a location called The Skull. (In Hebrew this place is called Golgotha.)

The Bible also verifies that Jesus was crucified at Calvary, in Luke23:33 (KJV) which states that

> And when they were come to the place, which is called Calvary, there they crucified him, and the malefactors, one on the right hand, and the other on the left.

God had planned for our Lord Jesus Christ to come and die for the sins of the world and our sins, that we all might be *saved*. It is because of this plan that God has ordained each of us to be free from the sins of the world. God has provided his only begotten Son, the Lord Jesus Christ, to be the one and only person by which we may be saved. Christ is our Redeemer, Our way back in the presence of God. It is the Spirit of God, the Holy Ghost, who reminds us that God is our redeemer.

> And they remembered that God was their rock, and the high God their redeemer. (Psalm 78:35, KJV)

It is by the power of the Holy Ghost that the saved people of God are able to recall the will of God. It is the will of God for us, the saved children of God, to be back in his presence. I pray in the name of Jesus Christ that we all become saved and enter back into the presence of our God.

> Remember the former things of old: for I am God, and there is none else; I am God, and there is none like me. (Isa. 46:9, KJV)

Remember God has a plan.
This is to glorify God. Amen!

HOW LONG IS ETERNITY

> God has revealed those things to us by his Spirit.
> —1 Corinthians 2:10 (GW)

It is to no end that eternity lends the answer to its length that becomes the beginning of the no end.

The Spirit reveals in the spelling of the word *eternity* these notions. The "E," entering the fullness of God when God's way began.

> The Lord already possessed me long ago, when his way began, before any of his works. (Prov. 8:22)

There was a notion given then that we are to fear the Lord and stay away from evil.

> So he told humans, The fear of the Lord is wisdom! To stay away from evil is understanding. (Job 28:28)

This understanding comes from the reading and studying of the Word of God. The notion behind (and for the representation) of the letter "T," which is the understanding of consciousness is in 1 Timothy 3:9 (God's Word Today's Translation).

It states,

> They must have clear consciences about possessing the mystery of the Christian faith.

Our faith is based on the foundation of Christ Jesus. This is the understanding we, as Christians, must know. It is because of our faith in the Son of God that we are saved.

> If you declare hat Jesus is Lord, and believe that God brought him back to life, you will be saved. (Rom. 10:9)

Here again, the notion of the letter "E" allows us the thought of *entering* into the fullness of God when his way began.

> The Lord already possessed me long ago when his way began, before any of his works. (Prov. 8:22)

It was God's plan from the beginning that we, through Jesus Christ, would be saved. Now this would become the way by which we become the children of God. The thought behind the letter "R" is *reality*, the revealed notion of God (Christ in the flesh). The Word was God in the flesh.

> In the beginning was the Word, and the Word was with God, and the Word was God. (John 1:1, KJV)

> And the Word was made flesh, and dwelt among us, and we beheld his glory, the glory as of the only begotten of the Father, full of grace and truth. (John 1:4, KJV)

This is the reality revealed by the Spirit that God himself put on flesh and came into the world for the purpose of redeeming us and making us his children. The notion of the letter "N" is revealed to stand for the *never-ending* knowledge of God that has not yet been revealed to man.

> For who hath known the mind of the Lord, that he may instruct him? But we have the mind of Christ. (1 Cor. 2:16, KJV)

Here it is revealed that the mind of God contains eternity. He created the place he dwells in the same way we build the space where our children play (the playground). God created eternity, the place where we, His children, shall play. Through death we shall travel out of time through space into eternity. We will travel out of the time that was set by the Father. This set time was for us to come to and pass through the Son in faith. But in order to enter into eternity, the place of his Holy Spirit, we must be transformed by the Holy Ghost. We will leave out from under the protection of the Father and travel through the Son by faith and be guided by the power of the Holy Ghost, who will guide, direct, and deliver our souls into eternity.

The notion revealed concerning the letter "I" is for entering *into* the realm of God's reality, which gave birth to the thought of salvation. This is a gift from God to men. This is the notion relating to the letter "T," which stands for *truth*.

> For the grace of God that bringeth salvation hath appeared to all men. (Titus 2:11, KJV)

Here we must understand that God makes us aware that it is only by His grace that we receive this gift. The "T" is the truth clearly stated in Titus 2:11.

The letter that represents the name of God is the letter "Y," which stands for *Yahweh*. This is the personal name of God in the Old Testament. It means *the Lord*. The name is a form of the Hebrew verb to be and most likely means *the One who is always present*. This meaning for the name Yahweh is found in the *Revell Bible Dictionary*. The notion of the "Y" is revealed to be the name *Yahweh*. The Alpha and the Omega, the Beginning and the End, God is, was, and will always be the One who is always present. God is eternal. He is without end. It is our God who has the answer to, "How long is eternity?"

This is to glorify God.

Amen!

I AM TO BECOME
THE INVISIBLE IMAGE OF GOD

> Who is the image of the invisible God, the
> firstborn of every creature.
> —Colossians 1:15 (KJV)

    I am the firstborn child of my mother—the first of all her creatures, the first of all her children. Within me is the invisible image of God. God created me in His own image to become like Christ—to become like the power of God.

> So God created man in his own image, in
> the image of God created he him; male and
> female created he them. (Gen. 1:27)

    God gave me his Spirit to live within me (the physical me). It is this Spirit that is the invisible image of God.

> Now we received, not the spirit of the world,
> but the spirit which is of God; that we might

> know the things that are freely given to us of
> God. (1 Cor. 2:12)

This Spirit is the life that I live in.

I am the mind, and my spirit is the life given to my mind that I, as the mind, become alive.

> And the Lord God formed man of the dust of the ground, and breathed into his nostrils the breath of life; and man became a living soul. (Gen. 2:7)

I am the created image of God. I am on earth to be educated on how to become like Christ.

> Let this mind be in you, which was also in Christ Jesus. (Phil. 2:5)

After giving your will to Christ, this is the mind we shall learn to receive. I was created and planted here on earth to learn of the power that is within me, to learn of God.

> And the Lord God planted a garden eastward in Eden; and there he put the man whom he had formed. (Gen. 2:8)

The power of God is eternally alive. The power within me is God. It is my life-giver. I am alive.

My spirit lives in Jesus Christ.

> And we know that the Son of God is come, and hath given us an understanding, that we may know him that is true, and we are in him that is true, even in his Son Jesus Christ. This is the true God, and eternal life. (1 John 5:20)

This is to glorify God!

I SHALL RECOVER IT ALL WITH FAITH

> For therein is the righteousness of God revealed from faith to faith: as it is written, The just shall live by faith.
> —Romans 1:17 (KJV)

The faith our Father God gave us, by which our faith in the name of the Son of God and this same faith is by which the Holy Ghost directs our path according to the will of God. I shall recover it all and become saved according to the will of God, for it is by God's will that I am to be saved.

> That if thou shalt confess with thy mouth the Lord Jesus, and shalt believe in thine heart that God hath raised him from the dead, thou shalt be saved. (Rom. 10:9, KJV)

This is God's promise on my life that I will return to God. I will have within me a renewed mind. I will become a recreated spirit to deliver God's Word to my soul, and I shall become a saved man of God in the name of the only begotten Son of God, my Lord Jesus Christ.

> And be not conformed to this world: but be ye transformed by the renewing of your mind that ye may prove what is that good, and acceptable, and perfect, will of God. (Rom. 12:2, kjv)

This promise is a gift from God that I am to come back to God the Father through faith in the Son of God, by being transformed by the Spirit of God, the Holy Ghost.

These three—the Father, the Son, and the Holy Ghost— are one idea for redemption. Meaning the three images of God is all used to save us.

> Neither by the blood of goats and calves, but by his own blood he entered in once into the holy place, having obtained eternal redemption for us. (Heb. 9:12, kjv)

Our Father gave us the faith. Our faith is to be used to believe in the Son. Because of our faith in Jesus Christ, the Holy Ghost will transform us to become like Christ—born of God.

> Which were born, not of blood, nor of the will of the flesh, nor of the will of man, but of God. (John 1:13, KJV)

> Whosoever is born of God doth not commit sin; for his seed remaineth in him: and he cannot sin, because he is born of God. (1 John 3:9, KJV)

In the beginning Adam (meaning us) was created by God. Jesus Christ was born of God from the beginning. A very person born from the created Adam is a created being of God in the likeness of God, yet still created. We must become born again in order to be like Christ and see the kingdom.

> Jesus answered and said unto him, Verily, verily, I say unto thee, Except a man be born again, and he cannot see the kingdom of God. (John 3:3, KJV)

This is done by accepting Jesus Christ as our Savior. We must believe, with the faith the Father gave us, that Jesus is Lord of our lives, and our faith in Jesus Christ is then used through the Son of God by the Holy Ghost as the faith that transforms us to become like Christ Jesus. Faith of the Father, faith of the Son, and faith of the Holy Ghost are one and the same, but used in three different images to direct us back in the presence of God.

> For there are three that bear record in heaven,
> the Father, the Word, and the Holy Ghost:
> and these three are one. (1 John 5:7, KJV)

The Bible goes on to speak of the three that are in the earth as a witness in the 1 John 5:8 (KJV) and it says,

> And there are three that bear witness in the earth, the Spirit, and the water, and the blood: and these three agree in one.

With faith in my life from the Father, I will always believe with faith in the Lord Jesus Christ, and that because of this faith the Holy Ghost will transform us all as believers to become like Christ.

> Whosoever believeth that Jesus is the Christ is born of God: and every one that loveth him that begat loveth him also that is begotten of him. (1 John 5:1, KJV)

We are to *believe* what the Father says. Our *belief* should be in the Son, and we, as the believers are whom the Holy Ghost shall transform.

This is God's promise for our lives. It is by the grace of the Trinity, by God that I am, and will always be truly, I mean, truly, truly saved

This is to glorify God!

I WOULD NOT BE IF IT WERE NOT FOR GOD

I was an alcoholic, drug addict, and smoker for twenty-six years of my life. Two guys tried to rob me and lost, and for this fight, I was arrested for assault. I stayed in jail for fifteen months and was released on three years supervised probation.

That was three years ago.

Today I am a man of God. I found God in jail. This was the best thing that I have ever uncovered—God is real. This I know for myself, for God chose me to reveal his glory in my life.

> Wherefore let them that suffer according to the will of God commit the keeping of their souls to him in well doing, as unto a faithful Creator. (1 Pet. 4:19)

If God had not created, I would not be, for I am the created Image of Him. I am the created likeness of God. This likeness is Spirit, for I am created in the Spirit, the likeness of God.

> So God created man in his own image, in the image of God created he him; male and female created he them. (Gen. 1:27)

I am the person that the spirit of God brought to life. I am the person who lives in the Spirit of God. It is the Spirit that gives me life. I am the person God created in his own image. This means that I am alive in the Spirit of God. This makes me a spiritual being.

> For in him we live, and move, and have our being; as certain also of your own poets have said, For we are also his offspring. (Acts 17:28)

God created me first within his Spirit then formed me a body, and then blew me into the body with his breath of life, and I became a living soul, a man of the dust of the earth that was now a man alive in the flesh.

> And the Lord God formed man of the dust of the ground, and breathed into his nostrils the breath of life; and man became a living soul. (Genesis 2:7)

The Spirit has revealed to me that God gave me a body to take in sin so that sin would never enter my spirit, for my spirit is of God. and in God there is no darkness at all.

There is no sin at all.

> This then is the message which we have heard of him, and declare unto you, that God is light, and in him is no darkness at all. (1 John 1:5)

God is Spirit, and the Spirit of God never dies. God protected me from sin in the beginning by creating me in the spirit. This is the place where God comes to talk to me.

> The Spirit itself beareth witness with our spirit, that we are the children of God. (Rom. 8:16)

The Spirit of God is my home. This is the place I shall live in for eternity. This place is in Christ Jesus, the brightness of God's glory.

> Who being the brightness of his glory, and the express image of his person, and upholding all things by the word of his power, when he had by himself purged our sins, sat down on the right hand of the Majesty on high. (Heb. 1:3)

The brightness of God's glory is light. This light has three images—the Father, the Word, and the Holy Ghost.

> For there are three that bear record in heaven, the Father, the Word, and the Holy Ghost: and these three are one. (1 John 5:7)

There is a male, a female, and a child. They are all of one spirit. This is how life is created. The likeness of God, the Father, and the Holy Ghost come together as one to create the one child known as God, the Word.

The Holy Ghost acts as the Mother who is the comforter, the bearer of the Word, the Child of God the Father.

> And there appeared a great wonder in heaven; a woman clothed with the sun, and the moon under her feet, and upon her head a crown of twelve stars: And she being with child cried, travailing in birth, and pained to be delivered. (Rev. 12:1–2)

This is how life for man is created—for man is created in the image of God, male and female.

This is how the child is brought forth: Physically and Spiritually.

God does things the same way all the time. He never Changes. The order of God remains the same. The Word, who is the seed of God the Father, is brought out of God through the Holy Spirit.

> In the beginning was the Word, and the Word was with God, and the Word was God. (John 1:1)

Again the Spirit reveals the Likeness of God: Male and Female, God the Father and the Holy Ghost, the Mother and the Word is Jesus the Christ, the Savor of Man, male and female and the children of them.

So you see, I would not be if it were not for God.

I thank you, Lord, for allowing my birth to happen.

I am Allen Brown, the person that lives in Christ. I am the eternal spiritual son of God, gifted with the Spirit of Christ, the spiritual son of God.

> And this is the record, that God hath given to us eternal life, and this life is in his Son. (1 John 5:11)

The Son of God is the Word that was with God, for the Word is the Beginning that is God.

> In the beginning was the Word, and the Word was with God and the Word was God. (John 1:1)

Thank you to all the children of God
This is to glorify God!

IN US (TRUST), THROUGH US (RUNS FAITH), AND OUT OF US (THE TRANSFORMATION)

> But mine eyes are unto thee, O Lord: in thee is my trust; leave not my soul destitute.
> —Psalm 141:8 (KJV)

In *us* there is a trust that we have in our Father. God's Word flows through us because of our faith in the Son of God.

> I am crucified with Christ: nevertheless I live; yet not I, but Christ liveth in me: and the life which I now live in the flesh I live by the faith of the Son of God, who loved me, and gave himself for me. (Gal. 2:20, KJV)

Out Of us, our transformation is revealed by the Holy Ghost as we are changed to become like Christ.

> Behold, I shew you a mystery; We shall not all sleep, but we shall all be changed. (1Cor. 15:51, KJV)

Being born again is what this part is called. It is called this because we are born of God when we profess the Lord Jesus Christ.

> Being born again, not of corruptible seed, but of incorruptible, by the word of God, which liveth and abideth forever. (1 Pet. 1:2, KJV)

Jesus was God because of the Christ that lived in him. God lived in the body of Jesus, making Jesus Christ the Son of God. Christ is the power of God revealed in Jesus. Jesus is the visual image of God in the flesh.

> Who is the image of the invisible God, the firstborn of every creature. (Col. 15:15, KJV)

> He is the image of the invisible God, the firstborn of all creation. (Col. 15:15, GW)

We must trust that we are *transformed*. We must trust the Father.
Trust.
We must have faith in the Son, and we must be transformed.

These are the three orders of God's promise. God's order is the Father, the Son, and the Holy Ghost.

God never changes!

God's promise is of the truth, his Spirit tells me so. I believe, because my faith was given to me by God so that I would trust God's truth, and that I would know God is God. God's promise is that I shall be (saved *through* faith) in his Son. The spirit of God, the Holy Ghost, it is He who transforms us to become like Christ Jesus, the very image of God. We are to put off the old man that was created and was led to sin. This is the man that is corrupted according to the deceitful lust in the created flesh, and this is by the corruption of sin.

> That ye put off concerning the former conversation the old man, which is corrupt according to the deceitful lusts. (Eph. 4:22, KJV)

I believe it is our duty to let the light of the Lord shine before men.

> Let your light shine before men, that they may see your good works, and glorify your Father which is in heaven. (Math. 5:16, KJV)

We must let go of the old man in order to live according to God's will, ready and able to release God's glory to the sons of men.

> And have put on the new man, which is renewed in knowledge after the image of him that created him. (Col. 3:10, KJV)

This is simply saying that we are re-created in the Spirit with a renewed mind full of the knowledge after the likeness of the image of God. With a renewed mind, we are to become aware that God will take care of us. God becomes the provider of all the things in our lives.

> The Lord is my light and my salvation; whom shall I fear? The Lord is the strength of my life; of whom shall I be afraid? (Ps. 1:1, KJV)

With God on your side, how is it possible to fail at anything?

Of course, we all know that God is the Creator of all there is, seen and unseen. We believers have the strength to trust and believe in the Father. We are saved through our faith, and through the Holy Ghost, we are restored back into the presence of God. What is in us is the trust of the Father. That which works through us is faith in the Son of God. And by the power of God's Spirit, the Holy Ghost, we are transformed to be like Christ.

> That the name of our Lord Jesus Christ may be glorified in you, and ye in him, according

to the grace of our God and the Lord Jesus Christ. (2 Thess. 1:12, kjv)

May he always be!
This is to glorify God!

LOOKING FOR THE WISDOM OF GOD

> He has reserved priceless wisdom for decent people.
> —Proverbs 2:6–7 (GW)

If you want the wisdom of God, you must repent of all your sins and give your life to Jesus Christ. Give your life to God and allow God's will to govern your life. You must do what Christ did for us. You must die to the things you know. You must lay down your old way of living and become born of God. Let the Spirit of God, The Holy Ghost, transform your spirit to be like Christ. The Spirit teaches your soul to be like Christ. This is the will of God for your life. God wants to adopt you. He wants you to become His child.

The wisdom of God is the Word, the Word that became human.

> The real light, which shines on everyone, was coming into the world. He was in the world, and the world came into existence through him. Yet, the world didn't recognize him. He went to his own people, and his

own people didn't accept him. However, he gave the right to become God's children to everyone who believed in him. (John 1:9–13, GW)

The light that shines on everyone is the Word.

> The Word became human and lived among us. We saw his glory. It was the glory that the Father shares with his only Son, a glory full of kindness and truth. (John 1:14, GW)

This is the wisdom of God that is stated in John 1:1 (GW) which says,

> In the beginning the Word already existed. The Word was with God, and the Word was God.

Here in this scripture, the word *word* is used three times, (meaning the Father, the Son, and the Holy Ghost). These three are one spiritual being. God is the Creator of all things, seen and unseen.

> He was the source of life, and that the life was the light for humanity. (John 1:4, GW)

The light that is for humanity is the Word, and the Word was with God, and the Word was God.

This is the wisdom of God given by divine inspiration. This is to glorify God! Amen!

LOVE CREATES, HATE DESTROYS

Love is like a crystal clear teardrop that came from being touched by God. Love is seen when the sun rises. It shows that the force of time is becoming life. Love is shown even in death. There is life in death. This life, which is its light, is propelled across the space that was once darkness. This light of life reveals the new life of God's glory. We are beings who are meant to become the children of God.

> For you are all children of the light and of the day; we don't belong to darkness and night. (1 Thess. 5:5, NLT)

In the acceptance of Christ as our Lord and Savior, we become the new life which is God's glory. We become the children of God.

> You are all children of God through faith in Christ Jesus. (Gal. 3:26, NLT)

Our light shines in the darkness of this world. We reveal the glory of God by allowing the light of the Lord in us to rise like the morning sun on the world around us. We are to and must speak of the goodness of God to everyone.

> But let us who live in the light think clearly, protected by the body armor of faith and love, and wearing as our helmet the confidence of our salvation. (1 Thess. 5:8, NLT)

This light is clearly the goodness of God that lives in us and should be kept apart from the darkness that wants to control us. There is something here that God wants to reveal.

> Then God said, "Let there be light," and there was light. And God saw that it was good. Then He separated the light from the darkness. (Gen. 1:3–4, NLT)

> In the beginning God created the heavens and the earth. (Gen. 1:1, NLT)

First, heaven here is the creation of space which is the second thing God created. Second, space is contained inside of time. Third, God created the beautiful earth.

Heaven is the space where the earth lives. This body and Earth is in space. It was placed in space by God in the beginning. What is the power that holds it there?

> The Son reflects God's own glory, and everything about him represents God exactly. He sustains the universe by the mighty power of his command. After he died to cleanse us from the stain of sin, he sat down in the place of honor at the right hand of the majestic God in heaven. (Hebrews 1:3, NLT)

It is by the power of Christ that the earth stays in place. Earth was created to perform and live inside of space. Space is the body that surrounds Earth. Time is the beginning God created where space lives in.

Why?

Because the Bible states that God created the beginning first.

> In the beginning God created. (Gen. 1:1)

That which was created in the beginning is time. Time is the body that surrounds space. The time it takes for the notion to be conceived, the thought is already telling us that there is something inside of time. For out of that time came space. This is clearly the order God gave creation in the beginning. Because a notion, a thought created, is contained inside of something, somewhere, and somehow. It must reveal itself according to the order of God. The something is time that the heaven is in. The garden of God is placed somewhere in heaven. The space that the earth is somehow held in is heaven. The garden of God is the earth. Space was placed inside of time so that man could, in death, travel the cold distance into eternity.

According to God's will and the time that God set for his eternal destination, man would, in time, come to believe in Christ and gain eternal life. Man must die to himself and live by faith in Christ.

> I assure you; those who listen to my message and believe in God who sent me have eternal life. They will never be condemned for their sins, but they have already passed from death into life. (John 5:25, NLT)

It is in time that we all die. This death or force of time is the way we are propelled into eternity. We pass through the space we occupy. We are the occupants of our body. Our bodies occupy the places we live here on planet Earth. It is here on Earth, the garden of God, that we were planted. It is here that we grow in the knowledge of God and die with the wisdom of God. So in death we are propelled by the force of time into eternity with the truth and understanding of God's promises for our salvation. The force of time is so great that we pass through space.

We arrive in eternity instantly. The force of time, death, is the way we are all to travel.

> When Adam sinned, sin entered the entire human race. Adam's sin brought death,

so death spread to everyone, for everyone sinned. (Rom. 5:12, NLT)

Our physical bodies were never meant to enter eternity. They are time capsules meant to allow us to become aware of God being active in our lives. God created us, so he knows us.

> I knew you before I formed you in your mother's womb. Before you were born I set you apart and appointed you as my spokesman to the world. (Jer. 1:5, NLT)

Once we became aware of the truth, the knowledge, wisdom, and understanding of God and accepted by faith, the Lord Jesus, we were to choose to repent of our sins and return to Him.

> For the wages of sin is death, but the free gift of God is eternal life through Christ Jesus our Lord. (Rom. 6:23, NLT)

God made sure that we would not have any excuses not to know of Him and of this free gift.

> "But this is the new covenant I will make with the people of Israel on that day," says the Lord. "I will put my laws in their minds, and I will write them on their hearts. I will

be their God, and they will be my people. And they will not need to teach their neighbors, nor will they need to teach their family, saying, 'You should know the Lord.' For everyone, from the least to the greatest, will already know me," says the Lord. "And I will forgive their wickedness and will never again remember their sins." (Jer. 31:33–34, NLT)

Now when our body dies, we will be propelled by the force of time most acridly across space into eternity from the earth, which is in space that is wrapped in time. The power that holds it all together is the Holy Spirit, who in the Name of Jesus Christ sustains it.

> The Son reflects God's own glory, and everything about him represents God exactly. He sustains the universe by the mighty power of his command. After he died to cleanse us from the stain of sin, he sat down in the place of honor at the right hand of the majestic God of Heaven. (Heb. 1:3, NLT)

When God's truth is known to us and we become aware that we are of Him and accept Him, then He will become our Lord.

> God alone made it possible for you to be in Christ Jesus. For our benefit God made Christ to be wisdom itself. He is the one who made us acceptable to God. He made us pure and holy, and he gave himself to purchase our freedom. (1 Cor. 1:30, NLT)

It is by this truth that we eagerly await the time that will come to release us from the space we occupy while in our bodies here on earth. This force of time, which is death, will propel us across space into eternity where we will see and will be judged by God.

This is to glorify God.

Amen!

LOVE IS THE LIFE THAT WE LIVE

> And thou shalt love the Lord thy God with all thine heart, and with all thy soul, and with all thy might.
> —Deuteronomy 6:5 (KJV)

Love is God. Love is the Father, and we Love God as our Father.

> And this is the record, that God hath given to us eternal life, and this life is in his Son. (1 John 5:11, KJV)

Life is the Christ.

> Now the birth of Jesus Christ was on this wise: When as his mother Mary was espoused to Joseph, before they came together, she was found with child of the Holy Ghost. (Matt. 1:18, KJV)

Live according to the Holy Ghost.

Live according to the Comforter, and the Holy Ghost will help you live the life you chose.

> In this was manifested the love of God toward us, because that God sent his only begotten Son into the world, that we might live through him. (1 John 4:9, KJV)

God becomes the Father who became the Christ (the Son), who was born through the Holy Ghost.

> In the beginning was the Word, and the Word was with God, and the Word was God. (1 John 1:1, KJV)

God is the Son who became, through the Holy Ghost, Jesus Christ, God in the Flesh. God is the Holy Ghost, the wonder-working power, who gave the seed of birth to Mary and created Jesus. The glory of it all is God's because God is love, because God gave us life, and because of God, we live.

God's order of perfection is seen in the number three (God's order) and the three images of God (the Father, the Son and the Holy Ghost). These are the three orders and images which God has revealed about Himself. Following this order and his images, God revealed to me that love is the life that we live.

The three L's—the Father *loves* the *life* given by the Son that we may *live* in faith through the Holy Ghost.

The Holy Ghost directs, guides, and teaches our spirit all the things that are of God. This is how we are to live. The Son of God gave his life and shed his blood that we might be forgiven as sinners. It is the blood of Christ Jesus that gave us a new life. God the Father lost his Son who became the payment for our sins.

> And he is the propitiation for our sins: and not for ours only, but also for the sins of the whole world. (1 John 2:2, KJV)

This was how much God loves us, and we are to love one another as much as God loved us. As Christians we are to Love the Lord Jesus Christ, the Son of God, all our physical Life with faith that God has given us through the Holy Ghost, who according to the will of God, will guard, guide, and govern the way we live.

According to the will of God we are to love one another as our selves through this life as we live in Christ.

The Bible says in the book of Romans 6:23 that

> For the wages of sin is death; but the gift of God is eternal life through Jesus Christ our Lord.

This is to glorify God!
Amen!

MAN IS THE SET HEAD

> I am crucified with Christ: nevertheless I live; yet not I, but Christ liveth in me: and the life which I now live in the flesh I live by the faith of the Son of God, who loved me, and gave himself for me.
> —Galatians 2:20 (KJV)

I am a man. I am the set head that God created in his own image. My spirit has never been seen (neither has God's spirit ever been seen). The set head of man is spiritual. He is only seen by God in the likeness of himself. This spirit of man is the created image of God himself.

Man's authority in the world is, as the set, that of a ruler (the man in charge). This position is first (just as how God is, was, and will always be number one).

God is the Father, the Son, and the Holy Ghost. Man is the created son of God that God chose to rule the world, but Satan stole man's ruling authority.

> [A]nd he did eat. (Gen. 3:6, KJV)

This is when Satan stole man's world, placed sin in it, and placed sin in man. God created the earth for man to rule upon, but man fell because of sin. The physical man will never rule the world, but the Spiritual Man (Jesus Christ) shall take it back and save it from sin.

> And if any man hears my words, and believes not, I judge him not: for I came not to judge the world, but to save the world. (John 12:47, kjv)

The Spiritual Man is the set head. I am talking about the man and the Lord Jesus Christ. I am the man that the Lord Jesus Christ lives in.

I am a child of God, Amen!

This is to glorify God!

WHAT GOD HAS DONE FOR ME
MY SOUL IS WHERE GOD'S SPIRIT LIVES

> And we know that the Son of God is come, and hath given us understanding, that we may know him that is true, and we are in him that is true, even in his Son Jesus Christ. This is the true God and eternal life.
> —John 5:20 (KJV)

What is *this* that is revealed as God?
It is Jesus Christ.

> All things are delivered unto me of my Father: and no man knoweth the Son, but the Father; neither knoweth any man the Father, save the Son, and he to whomsoever the Son will reveal him. (Matthew 11:27)

The Spirit of God is what makes my soul alive. God lives in me, and I live in him. As long as God's Spirit is in me, I will live forever—this is the will of God for my life. I, through faith, believe God.

> That if thou shalt confess with thy mouth the Lord Jesus, and shalt believe in thine heart that God hath raised him from the dead, thou shalt be saved. (Romans 10:9)

I see my soul before God as light without life. Then God gives me a part of his Spirit, a unique individual spirit that makes me me. This spirit is what brings me to life.

> And the Lord God formed man of the dust of the ground, and breathed into his nostrils the breath of life; and man became a living soul. (Gen. 2:7)

God and I will always be together. I am grateful that God called me to become a child of his.

I thank God!

The Bible reveals in Romans 8:16 that

> The Spirit itself beareth witness with our spirit, that we are the children of God.

This I am—a soul without life. God gave me his Spirit, and it brought me to life. Now my soul and God's Spirit are what brought me to life. This life is God in me, for God is life. I live because of God, and I live with God, for I was created in the image of God.

> So God created man in his own image, in the image of God created he him; male and female created he them. (Genesis 1:27)

My life is God's. This part of God that lives in me is a gift from God that created life in me . I am alive in the image of God.

The Bible says in the book of Ephesians 2:8 that, "For by grace are ye saved through faith; and that not of yourself: it is the gift of God."

I am a spiritual soul that will live forever with God. Amen!

This is to glorify God!

TO WHOM MUCH IS GIVEN, MUCH IS REQUIRED

What God has planned for *you* from the beginning is for *you* (who has come to be with God) to share the things of God with others who have also come to believe in Him.

From the very beginning God had you. This means you were with God, and God was with you.

> In the beginning was the Word, and the Word was with God, and the Word was God. (John 1:1, KJV)

The beginning was what God had created for you. This was your process of becoming like the Word. The word *origin*, *beginning*, or genesis is the first order of time. The first thing God did was to create you. *Create* means to bring into being (this is according to *Webster's Basic Dictionary*). The first thing God did was to call *you* into being. God created your soul.

> So God created man in his own image, in the image of God created he him; male and female created he them. (Genesis 1:27, KJV)

Here we see that God called us to be with him. He created us, and He called us into our existence. Then the second thing God did was to form you. We were with Him when he made our body from the dust of the ground. Much like how man makes a car, God created the soul and gave it a body. The car can't operate by itself. It needs a driver. The body can't perform without an operator. The operator of the body is the soul, which is us, the being.

> And the Lord God formed man of the dust of the ground, and breathed into his nostrils the breath of life; and man became a living soul. (Genesis 2:7, KJV)

The driver can not operate the car without gas. Much like the soul can't operate the body without the Breath of life—this is the third thing God did when he created you. So God blew the breath of life into the body just as someone gasses up a car in order for the operator to move the car or for the car to run.

Now that the body has life just as the car now has gas, the soul can now operate the body in this world just as the driver can now drive the car. You see, the soul is our spiritual beginning. It knows, chooses, and feels the Spirit of God. Without the body, it knows nothing of the world.

There was a problem in the world called sin. God created a plan to rid the world of this sin.

> For the Lord of hosts hath purposed, and who shall disannul it? And his hand is stretched out, and who shall turn it back? (Isaiah 14:27, kjv)

It is with this hand that God created the body. Each of us is a part of the body of Christ. This body which belongs to Jesus Christ (for He is the head) came into the world to rid the world of sin.

> For then must he often have suffered since the foundation of the World: but now once in the end of the world hath he appeared to put away sin by the sacrifice of himself. (Hebrews 9:26, kjv)

Christ did this of his own free will.

> No man taketh it from me, but I lay it down of myself. I have power to take it again. This commandment have I received of my Father. (John 10:18, kjv)

To Him much was given because all things were created for Him, through Him, and by Him, *so much was required of Him.* We who are born of Him are kept by Him.

> Who are kept by the power of God through faith unto salvation ready to be revealed in the last time. (1 Peter 1:5, KJV)

All things are kept by His Power. From the beginning He chose to suffer for the world. The place where we live, He Lives. This is why God loved the world. This world was created to be a garden.

> The cedars in the garden of God could not hide him: the fir trees were not like his boughs, and the chestnut trees were not like his branches; nor any tree in the garden of God was like unto him in his beauty. (Ezekiel 31:8, KJV)

Yes, it is here in this beautiful world, the garden of God, where God would plant us as created beings like seeds. We come from God above and are planted here in the world to grow. Here, we would grow and become his children.

> He that cometh from above is above all: he that is of the earth is earthly, and speakth of the earth; he that cometh from heaven is above all. (John 3:31, KJV)

Through the, and by, the discernment of the Spirit, we see here that God reveals why he loves the world. The world was to be the place where He would reveal his love as a Father for his Son.

> The Father loveth the Son and hath given all things into his hand. (John 3:35, KJV)

Through the power of his Holy Spirit will He guide, guard, and protect his children until they are ready. (They, of their own free will, have willingly learned and accepted the wisdom, knowledge, and understanding of God until they grow to believe).

> He that believeth on the Son hath everlasting life: and he that believeth not the Son shall not see life; but the wrath of God abideth on him. (John 3:36)

Until they believe this with faith, only then would they be ready to come home into eternity and live forever in the love of God. He would plant us like seeds in the earth, and He would watch us grow and become his children. It is for this reason and this reason alone, that God loves the world.

> For God so loved the world, that he gave his only begotten Son, that whosoever

believeth in him should not perish, but have everlasting life. (John 3:16)

God allowed us in sin that we might believe in Christ and also be saved and redeemed. His gift of grace was given to all men for salvation. Our human bodies are the vessels we operate in this world of sin while on our journey to salvation, which was accomplished on our behalf by our Lord Christ Jesus. Clearly salvation is the work of God's grace, for He alone is to be praised.

This is to glorify God.

Amen!

OF WHOM I SPEAK, HE IS THE BEGINNING

> In the beginning God created the Heavens and the Earth.
>
> —Genesis 1:1 (KJV)

The first thing God did was to create. Out of Himself, he called forth the beginning. He created time. The second thing God did was to create the heavens, the space that contain the elements of materials. The third thing God did was to create the earth. The Earth is made of material matter, a planet in the total material universe, a solid form of matter. The first two creations were not seen and could not be touched, but are just as real as the third creation. This creation—the earth—is touchable and seen.

Something to think about: our soul cannot be seen and neither can our spirit, but our body can be seen and is touchable. So here we see that God created time, space, and matter. These three were created by the order of God. God performs in the same order, all the time. The order of God is the Father, the Son, and the Holy Spirit. This order is the stamp of God's perfection. This is the image in which God chose to reveal His glory. God is the same God yesterday, today, and tomorrow. The spiritual home of God, heaven, is the realm where God lives.

> And he said unto them, When ye pray, say, Our Father which art in *heaven*, Hallowed be thy name. Thy kingdom come. Thy will be done, as in heaven, so in earth. (Luke 11:2, KJV; italics added)

Then if the home of God is heaven, which is the place where He lives, so then heaven exists within us. When we pray, we are to within ourselves ask God to keep Himself holy in us as we live out our daily lives here on earth. We are to pray that nothing we do contaminates His being while He comes to lives in us, His kingdom.

> Neither shall they say, Lo here! Or lo there! For, behold, the kingdom of God is within you. (Luke 17:21, KJV)

This is done as we come to accept Christ Jesus as the Lord of our lives. The spirituality of God that lives in us is to be shown throughout the earth. It is to be shown in a way that reflects the glory of God that lives in us.

"Our Father" (is God)—this statement lets us know that we are chosen to be His children and are to ask of God's permission.

"Which art in heaven" says to us that God the Father is within us.

"Hallowed be thy name"—we are asking God to keep Himself holy while within us.

"Thy kingdom come"—we are asking God's permission to come into His presence.

"Thy will be done, as in heaven"—we are asking God to allow our spiritual nature to be led by the Holy Spirit, the nature, the will of God.

"So in earth"—So as we are led by the Spirit. we should lead by the Spirit.

Lives that reflect the glory of God while we're here in the earth.

Genesis means beginning, the first order of things. So the first thing we are to do is to take the time, which is the first of God's creation, to learn how to understand God's love for us. We are to give a testimony that will bring honor and glory to God. God created time for us to use to glorify Him in honor for this great love He has for us. So now the second thing the Lord God created was the heavens, which is space, and it was created in us as the places where God chooses to dwell. Now after comprehending His love and giving testimony about it, we should give praise and worship to Him.

Great love He has for us.

The third thing God did was to create our beautiful planet. God placed us here on Earth, and it is here that we should reflect the image of God's love to one another. These three things God did in the beginning, according to the order of the beginning.

> In the beginning God created the heaven
> and the earth. (Genesis 1:1)

Here we see that God created three things—time, space, and matter. God created the beginning (time), then God created the heavens (space), and third, God created the Earth (matter). He created, formed, and blew the breath of life into man, and man became a living being. These three acts were the order by which God created man.

> So God created man in his own image, in
> the image of God created he him; male and
> female created he them. (Genesis 1:27)

First, God created. He called the soul into existence. Second, the Lord God formed. He shaped man's body. Third, God breathed the breath of life into the man. God gave the man a part of Himself, which is a unique and a one-of-a-kind Spirit. This Spirit would posses its own free will that was to be led by the Holy Ghost.

> And the Lord God formed man of the dust
> of the ground, and breathed into his nostrils
> the breath of life; and man became a living
> soul. (Genesis 2:7)

This *breath* that was given to each of us as a gift from God is a freewill spirit. Our free will is specifically tuned to the voice of God. We all have the same spirit, but our spirits are set at a variety of different frequencies. We all hear His voice at different times and in different places, but we hear different things.

> Surely it is God's Spirit within people, the breath of the Almighty within them that makes them intelligent. (Job 32:8, NLT)

This is why we can pick up the Bible and read the same scripture and receive different messages. God reveals his will to each of our spirits according to who His will is directed at, for, and to. He chooses to use us to reveal His glory.

There are three images that direct us in what path we should allow our will to follow.

Number one, our will should be directed at the Father in love.

> And he answering said, Thou shalt love the Lord thy God with all thy heart, and with all thy soul, and with all thy strength, and with all thy mind; and thy neighbor as thyself. (Luke 10:27, KJV)

Number two, because of the Father's love that is always directed at us—His children. We follow this example by showing our love for the Son.

> Jesus answered and said unto him, If a man love me, he will keep my words: and my Father will love him, and we will come unto him, and make our abode with him. (John 14:23, kjv)

This is confirmation that the Lord God chose us to be His dwelling place.

Number three, our will was not meant to trust the things of the flesh. It was meant to enjoy the spiritual things of God. It is to trust to be guided, trained, and developed by the Holy Spirit.

> For the kingdom of God is not meat and drink; but righteousness, peace, and joy in the Holy Ghost. (Romans 14:17, kjv)

The material things of this world should not cause our will to go against the will of God for our lives. I pray that we realize the beautiful spiritual gifts of God that bring real joy and peace.

> May God, who gives this patience and encouragement, help you in complete harmony with each other—each with the attitude of Christ Jesus toward the other. Then all of you can join together with one voice, giving praise and glory to God the

Father of our Lord Jesus Christ. (Romans 15:5–6, NLT)

This is to glorify God.
Amen!

ONE MIND
ONE GOAL, ONE BODY, ONE SOUL

> For in him dwelleth all the fullness of the Godhead bodily.
>
> —Colossians 2:9 (KJV)

God has one goal as a Father. That is to make one Body for his only begotten Son, which will have one soul guided by the Holy Ghost.

All of God lives in Christ's body. We, the children of God (collectively), are the body of Christ. God lives in all of us .We are one body in Christ. This is true of those of us who are believers in the Lord Jesus Christ. The goal of the Father was to provide a body that his Son could reveal His glory through and reveal to us that we are of God.

> In this was manifested the love of God toward us, because that God sent his only begotten Son into the world, that we might live through him. (1 John 4:9, KJV)

As we, the body of Christ, live with faith in Christ, God reveals his glory through Christ, who lives in us, to the world. The body of Christ was to be created in the image of God.

> So God created man in his own image, in the image of God created he him; male and female created he them. (Genesis 1:27, KJV)

So the Godhead created man, and man became a living soul. The Father, the Son and the Holy Ghost are of one mind. So from the command of the Godhead, the first created soul was called by the name of Adam. Eve was a part of the body of Adam, just as we are a part of the body of Christ. Out of the flesh of Adam, Eve came sinless into the world so that in the flesh the Son of God would also come sinless into the world. This was done before sin had entered Adam. Eve was not told by God not to eat of the tree. It was the command given to Adam—the one soul, the one person, through which sin came to all mankind. But Adam was not the person through which sin entered the world. This was Lucifer. He placed sin in the world.

> Thou wast perfect in thy ways from the day that thou wast created, till iniquity was found in thee." (Ezekiel 28:15, KJV)

It is in this scripture that the Spirit reveals that Lucifer, Satan brought iniquity or sin into the world. Satan,

Lucifer, was created long before the one body—Adam—was created. Although Eve was deceived first, that is not what is really important. What's important is the fact God recognized Adam's failure as what allowed sin in man.

Not in the world but in men.

> And the Lord God called unto Adam, and said unto him, Where art thou? (Genesis 3:9, KJV)

Eve would be the key that would open the door through which the Son of God would be brought into the world. The one true God reveals this in Genesis 3:15.

> And I will put enmity between thee and the woman, and between thy seed and her seed; it shall bruise thy head, and thou shalt bruise his heel.

This is the foretelling of the arrival of the Lord Jesus. Jesus Christ was coming to take back the stolen authority over man, from Satan, and would free man from the enslavement of sin. The one soul would become free, free to accept and experience the awesome spiritual wisdom, knowledge, and understanding of the Godhead (one mind). The reason for the arrival of Jesus Christ (one soul), who embodies all of the children of God (those of us who believe), was to get ride of the devil's work, sin.

> He that committeth sin is of the devil; for the devil sinneth from the beginning. For this purpose the Son of God was manifested, that he might destroy the works of the devil. (1John 3:8, KJV)

The One Soul has come. He is Jesus Christ, and he's been given the body required to contain the fullness of God, and it has been guided, guarded, and proclaimed blameless in the eyes of the Godhead (one mind). The *one goal* of the Father was to sacrifice the one body of his only begotten Son so that we, the children of God, would have our one soul changed transformed and reborn of God by that awesome power of the Holy Ghost.

This is to glorify God.

Amen!

OUR FIGHT IS NOT WITH EACH OTHER

> This is my commandment, that ye love one another, as I have loved you
> —John 15:12 (KJV)

God gave us to one another to love each other, just as He, Himself, loves us.

This never-ending spirit of love as stated in John 15:12 was placed in each of us when our God blew the breath of life into our nostrils.

The Hebrew word for *breath* is ruach (רוּחַ) which means wind, breath, and spirit.

This spirit of love was placed in us.

> And the Lord God formed man of the dust of the ground, and breathed into his nostrils the breath of life; and man became a living soul. (Genesis 2:7, KJV)

This breath, this spirit of love, is a command given to us by God for us to love each other.

> These things I command you, that ye love one another. (John 15:17, KJV)

God made us to love one another. He put His Spirit of love in us, so by faith we should understand that we can, and do, love each other. It is not us we fight against. The anger that gets into us is not from the Spirit of God.

God is love.

This hostile force comes to attack the love we have for each other. It is not the person who love us that attacks us, but the power of principalities, our archenemy, Satan.

If we keep the command God gave, which is to love one another, we can together rebuke Satan, and he will flee, leaving us with the love that God gave us to share with each other.

> Submit yourselves therefore to God. Resist the devil, and he will flee from you. (James 4:7, KJV)

If we stop to see who our real enemy is when the attack comes, we would not battle against each other. We would fight together by praying and rebuking our common enemy. It is not the person before you, the One who loves you.

He or she is not your enemy.

Something enters each of us in anger—a spirit. Its purpose is to destroy the love that we share with one another. It comes like a thief.

> Submit yourselves therefore to God. Resist the devil, and he will flee from you. (James 4:7, KJV)

The Bible talks about this spirit as being a thief in John 10:10 saying, "The thief cometh not, but for to steal, and to kill, and to destroy: I am come that they might have life, and that they might have it more abundantly."

This spirit, This thief, is Satan. He is the enemy that we fight against. Not our loved ones. It's the spirit of Satan. It is this spirit that's found its way into our loved ones' open door of emotional frustration. Once he is in, he blinds them with feelings that corrupt their spiritual nature. We get mad at each other and can't see that it is he, the thief, that has come to destroy the love we have for one another. Blinded by our emotions, we call out names and use words that hurt each other. These are the times we are to pray with and for one another. We are to believe and trust in the spirit of love that God himself has placed in each of us. Jesus Christ is the source of our love.

> Herein is love, not that we loved God, but that he loved us, and sent his Son to be the propitiation for our sins. (1 John 4:10, KJV)

That's the love that comes from God who commands us to love each other. If God loves us enough to die for us and His Spirit of love lives in us, then we should be able to love one another no matter what our indifferences might be.

> Herein is love, not that we loved God, but that he loved us, and sent his Son to be the propitiation for our sins. (1 John 4:10, KJV)

> Beloved, let us love one another: for love is of God; and every one that loveth is born of God, and knoweth God. (1 John 4:7, KJV)

> Beloved, if God so loved us, we ought also to love one another. (1 John 4:11, KJV)

It is not the one you care about that does not care about you, it's that thief, that spirit, that walks the earth to and fro looking to devour what it may.

> And the Lord said unto Satan, Whence comest thou? Then Satan answered the Lord, and said, from going to and fro in the earth, and from walking up and down in it. (Job 1:7, KJV)

This foul spirit of the devil, Satan, in times has touched all of us in one way or another.

> [W]herein in time past ye walked according to the prince of the power of the air, the

spirit that now worketh in the children of
disobedience. (Ephesians 2:2, KJV)

Here you see that the spirit of Satan gets inside of people. He starts and causes confusion in the mind. We must understand that we were not created to destroy each other; we were meant to love one another.

> Be ye therefore followers of God, as dear children; and walk in love as Christ also hath loved us, and hath given himself for us an offering and a sacrifice to God for a sweetsmelling savor. (Ephesians 5:1–2, KJV)

You are to fight against the unseen principalities by listening to your spiritual nature and by allowing the Holy Spirit to control and guide you. We are not to take vengeance on each other.

> Dearly beloved, avenge not yourselves, but rather give place unto wrath: for it is written, Vengeance is mine; I will repay, saith the Lord. (Romans 12:19, KJV)

Always pray when under attack. Put on the armor of God. Remember, the person you love and care for is not the enemy; it is that thief, the spirit of the devil, that comes to destroy the love God has placed in you to be shared with the one you have feelings for. Remind your love one that the love of God lives in and that if the two of you pray together, together the two of you will stay.

So pray without ceasing and wear God's armor as it says in God's word.

> Put on the whole armor of God, that ye may be able to stand against the wiles of the devil. (Ephesians 6:11, KJV)

You, as a believer, must know, trust, and believe, that greater is he that lives in you than He that is in the world. You, as the believer, must know the Father. You must trust in the Son, and you must believe by faith that the Holy Spirit shall perform God's will in your life. God's Word was sent forth with orders for your life. These orders were carried, guarded, and delivered by the Holy Ghost. It was He who planted the Word of God into the womb of the Virgin Mary. This was the order that was sent for your life. Christ came so that you might have everlasting life in him.

> For God so loved the world, that he gave his only begotten Son, that whosoever believeth in him should not perish, but have ever lasting life. (John 3:16, KJV)

So remember, we are not to fight against each other. God's command is for us to love one another.

This is to glorify God. Amen!

OUT OF THE SOUL OF MAN COMES THE LIGHT OF THE LORD

> In the beginning God created the heaven and the earth.
>
> —Genesis 1:1 (KJV)

In the beginning, God created the beginning (time) in darkness. I say this because the next thing God did was create the heavens (space). If we look at space without the sun, moon, and stars, there is only darkness.

> And God made two great lights; the greater light to rule the day, and the lesser light to rule the night: he made the stars also. (Genesis 1:16, KJV)

Then the Bible says that God created the earth (matter). I believe that the Spirit is revealing to me that out of the darkness came the light. Here also, the Spirit is revealing the soul to be of the darkness. God knows the beginning and the end, so I say out of the soul of the Man came the light of the Lord. God called man into existence, and out of this void of darkness that he had created, the light came out of God.

God created man's soul. It was dark, so God placed the image of his own Spirit in the soul of the man. This spirit made man an individual. This Spirit is how man would know God. This is the first image of God the Father, and man was brought to life with emotions and consciousness. Man has been given free will, the ability to choose. The Bible states that God created a body for the man in Genesis 2:7.

> And the Lord God formed man of the dust of the ground, and breathed into his nostrils the breath of life; and man became a living soul. (Genesis 2:7, KJV)

Man now lives in a body with a soul that can feel the world that God created for him to grow and come to know God. This Earth is the garden of God. We were placed here by God and are given the opportunity to become the children of God. There is a third thing that God gave man. It's stated in the second part of the scripture in Genesis 2:7.

God blew from his own Spirit the breath of life into the spirit God placed in the soul of man, and man became a living soul in the image of God. The images of God are the Father (the spirit of man), the Son (in the likeness of the body of man), and the Holy Ghost (the renewed soul of the transformed man of God). These are the three images of God seen and unseen. We are created in the image of God.

> So God created man in his own image, in the image of God created he him; male and female created he them. (Genesis 1:27, KJV)

The soul of man is created after the likeness of God. Man is the soul who God called Adam. A spirit was given to man. It was placed in the soul of man.

> Now we have received, not the spirit of the world, but the spirit which is of God; that we might know the things that are freely given to us of God. (1 Corinthians 2:12, KJV)

The spirit is what gave the soul the ability to have a consciousness, emotions, and free will. I believe the Spirit is revealing to me that the soul and spirit were once one in the beginning when God first called the man into existence.

> But God hath revealed them unto us by his Spirit: for the Spirit searcheth all things, yea, the deep things of God. (1 Corinthians 2:10, KJV)

God is a spiritual being, so I say what God called came to him in his likeness, a soul filled with the Spirit of God, sinless and without flesh.

> And the Lord God formed man of the dust of the ground, and breathed into his nostrils

> the breath of life; and man became a living
> soul. (Genesis 2:7, KJV)

Once God created the flesh of the man, he then blew the breath of life into the body of the man. This was God blowing his Spirit into our bodies, and man became a living soul searching for the will of God for his life. I am that I am—the soul that God called me to be, but it is the spirit that God chose for me that allowed me to live for eternity.

> For the wages of sin is death; but the gift of
> God is eternal life through Jesus Christ our
> Lord. (Romans 6:23, KJV)

Not because of anything I have done.
God *chose* me before the creation of the world.
Amen! Glory to God!

Man was created without sin. God made man. Here is where I am able to understand that man was never born. Man was created by God to become an adopted child of God in the future.

> The Spirit itself beareth witness with our
> spirit, that we are the children of God.
> (Romans 8:16, KJV)

But as we know, sin came to destroy man and to stop man from becoming a child of God. Unknowingly, sin was the cause of man becoming a child of God. For without sin, man may not have had the opportunity to become a child of God. It is because of Adam's disobedience that we are born in sin. God gave Adam a command, and Adam disobeyed.

> But of the tree of the knowledge of good and evil, thou shall not eat of it: for in the day that thou eatest thereof thou shalt surely die. (Genesis 2:17)

It is because we are born in sin and because of God's grace and mercy that allowed us to the overcome sin. This is why God allows men to become his children. We are born again through faith in Jesus Christ. We are rewarded for the overcoming of the sin and saved through our faith in the Lord Jesus Christ. Man must accept the gift of faith in the Lord Jesus Christ to become a child of God.

> That if thou shalt confess with thy mouth the Lord Jesus, and shalt believe in thine heart that God hath raised him from the dead, thou shalt be saved. (Romans 10:9, KJV)

The soul of man is back in darkness because of Adam's disobedience. God has separated himself from man, meaning God divided the soul from the spirit, man died.

Man was separated from the Spirit of God. Man died spiritually. The soul and spirit separated.

This is what it meant in Genesis 2:17 when God said, "Thou shalt surely die."

The gift of the Spirit still lives in the man but not in man's soul. The soul and spirit share closeness side by side in the man. This means God has never really left man. God just separated his Spirit from the spirit of man by taking the spirit of man out of man's soul dividing the two within the man. This mystery is revealed to God's children.

> Even the mystery which hath been hid from ages and from generations, but now is made manifest to his saints. (Colossians 1:26, KJV)

See it like this, I am that I am—me—the image of myself. These are the three that I see are me. I create my image, outside myself, a look-alike.

First, like the Father, I put part of me in the created image. Step Two, the Son is the created image. And thirdly, to bring him to life, my look-alike, I breathe the image of myself in Spirit, the Holy Ghost, into the created image, and it becomes alive. This is what I receive when I read the scripture in the book of Genesis 1:27 and Genesis 2:7.

I pray that you of the Spirit of God are blessed to see what the Spirit of God is revealing. That out of the soul of man that was created and brought forth from the darkness that God created, comes the light of the Lord. It is not that we have chosen God, but God chose to allow Christ to live in us that we might bring forth more fruit unto God (more children). As we, with faith, accepted the Lord Jesus Christ as our Lord and Savior, this light is now the life of Christ that lives in us. It shines through us on the world around us. It shines on the unbelievers in this world. This light is a beacon that draws all men unto God.

> As long as I am in the world, I am the light of the world. (John 9:5, KJV)

This light, that is Christ, is how we as Christians are able to be fruitful and become fishers of men. We are the ones who God gives gifts to. We help reveal his will for other men. To inspire other people to accomplish the jobs that God has for their lives. Yes, the light of the Lord is Jesus Christ who lives in us the believers on the promises of God.

> But the scripture hath concluded all under sin, that the promise by faith of Jesus Christ might be given to them that believe. (Galatians 3:22, KJV)

We, as believers of the promises of God, shall live forever with God in heaven as the children of God.

For yea are all the children of God by faith in Christ Jesus. (Galatians 3:26, kjv)

This is to glorify God!
Amen!

PERFECTION—THE NUMBER THREE

> In the beginning God created the heaven and the earth.
> —Genesis 1:1 (KJV)

All of us read this verse and see the words in this format. We hear the sounds of the words as we read, but what are the hidden messages for us as individuals? What the Holy Spirit is revealing to us are messages for us to tell to the world. We are to reveal God's glory that lives in us to the world. The Holy Spirit will reveal its messages through us. We all receive a different and specific message. God has a specific calling for each of us. He has given each of us a special peace of Himself that belongs only to the individual. This is the peace of His spirit that makes us one-of-a-kind. We each have a spiritual part of God that makes us unique.

God has hidden the key to His messages for each of us in our spirit.

> God has revealed those things to us by his spirit. The spirit searches everything,

> especially the deep things of God. (1 Corinthians 2:10)

The key is our individuality. As we are led by the Holy Spirit, the spirit of God reveals God's message to our spirit who let's our soul know the things of God.

As the verse is read, "In the beginning God created the heaven and the earth," the point God makes me see is the order of perfection—the number three.

The order of God is always the same. God is, God was, and God will always be perfectly holy in all three images. The Father, the Son, and the Holy Spirit are the three images in which we see God's order of perfection. So in the beginning God created a beginning and middle and an end for us. God did this in the likeness of His divine order— past, present, and future.

> In the beginning the Word *already existed*. The Word *was with God*, and the *Word was God*. (John 1:1; italics added)

Here is the beginning of God's way concerning us.

Proverbs 8:22, "The Lord possessed me long ago, when his way began, before any of his works."

So God created time. God called time into existence first.

> In the beginning, God created the heaven
> and the Earth. (Genesis 1:1)

The first order of business, God created the beginning (is time). Now because of time we can begin to see the threefold nature of God.

The first nature, which is the calling of the Father, found in John 1:2.

> The same was in the beginning with God.
> (John 1:2)

Time came by way of the Father, who is the first person of the Godhead. The second person of the Godhead is the Son, who is the second image of God. He brought forth the heaven.

> Everything came into existence through
> him. (John 1:3)

The third person of the Godhead is the Holy Spirit.

> Not one thing that exists was made without
> him. (John 1:3)

He is the power that was used through the son to bring the earth into existence. The threefold nature of God can be thought of as the Word as stated in John 1:1–3.

> His Son is the reflection of God's glory and the exact likeness of God's being. (Hebrews 1:3)

We are created in the image of God in the likeness of Him. Our bodies are formed according to the second order of God's image, which is the Son. Jesus Christ was the house of the Lord, the body in which God lived in when He walked the earth.

(Just as our soul lives in our physical bodies.)

> God was pleased to have all of himself live in Christ. (Colossians 1:19)

> In the past God hid this mystery, but now he has revealed it to his people. God wanted his people throughout the world to know the glorious riches of this mystery-which is Christ living in you, giving you the hope of glory. (Colossians 1:26–27)

So here we see the truth in God's Word. Christ lives in us. If you want Christ to live in you just, do as Romans 10:9 says.

> If you declare that Jesus is Lord, and believe that God brought him back to life, you will be saved. (Romans 10:9)

The third part of a man is his spirit. This is found in Genesis 2:7.

We are unique individuals with a specific spirit. This is a special part of God that lives in us. This is according to the third order of the threefold nature of God. This is the Holy Spirit, who is the third image of God. It is by the Holy Spirit that our spirit receives the messages that God has for each of us. The Holy Spirit is truth. He is the key to understanding the messages of God. The Holy Spirit guides and teaches us according to God's will for our life. We have three images in the likeness of the threefold nature of God himself.

God created all of us according to this number of perfection—the number three. The three points of perfection that God created are the soul, the body, and the spirit, which are literally in this order. When God created man, he first called the man's soul into existence. Then God shaped the man's body from the dust of the earth. Third, He blew the breath of life into the nostrils of man placing apart of his spirit into man causing him to become a living being. As I read Genesis 1: 27 the Spirit reveals to me, this is the mark of perfection. This was done so that we could learn, grow and come to know him. Once we learn to fear God, we grow in the knowledge and understanding of Him, then we can express the wisdom of God by accepting Jesus Christ as our Lord and Savior. This is how we can come to know him through the acceptance of Jesus Christ we can stand in the presence of God. The threefold order and nature of God is always the same image according to the Father, the Son, and the Holy Spirit. The mark of perfection is the number three.

This is to glorify God
Amen!

REALITY CHECK

> For there are three that bear record in heaven, the Father, the Word, and the Holy Ghost: and these three are one.
>
> —1 John 5:7 (KJV)

There is a reality between the Father, the Son, and the Holy Ghost. The reality is they are all God.

There is a reality between the mind, the soul, and the brain. The reality is they are all me—man.

And there is a reality between God, me, and the devil, and this reality is, between the two, I am the chosen one.

> Whosoever is born of God doth not commit sin; for his seed remaineth in him: and he cannot sin, because he is born of God. (1 John 3:9)

This is my reality with God. I am the chosen child of God. The reality is that I was chosen by God because of my faith in the Lord Jesus Christ—or am I of the devil.

> He that committeth sin is of the devil; for the devil sinneth from the beginning, For this purpose the Son of God was manifested, that he might destroy the works of the devil. (1 John 3:8)

The choice was given to me from God himself. I am to choose out of my own free will between God or the devil. This plan was God's from the beginning.

How were we to become the children of God?

In Proverbs 8:22 God's wisdom spoke, it said,

> The Lord possessed me in the beginning of his way, before his works of old.

This was when God's way began for the thought and creation of man. A tool was needed to produce sin in man, this tool was Lucifer.

> This tells that God created Lucifer with iniquity within himself and that Lucifer would at one moment in time give birth to sin. (Ezekiel 28:15, KJV)

The Bible reveals it like this in the book of Romans 8:19 which says, "For the earnest expectation of the creature waiteth for the manifestation of the sons of God."

Lucifer was the tool needed to put the sin in man. The Bible say in Romans 8:20 that

> For the creature was made subject to vanity, not willingly, but by reason of him who hath subjected the same in hope.

God created Lucifer perfect with all of the bad stuff needed to tempt man and entice man to become a sinner. This sin in men would be the fall of man. My inside man sees God's love fighting to be loved by me, for it is love that needs to be loved.

> Beloved, let us love one another: for love is of God; and every one that loveth is born of God, and knoweth God. (1 John 4:7)

I believe the Spirit is revealing God's love for us.

How would we know how to love God and understand the fullness of God without knowing sin?

Without pain, how would we understand joy?

God is the same all the time. God is life, love, and light. Life is eternal, Love is everlasting, and God is the light of men. When God's way began, God chose man to become his child. There is a scripture in the Bible that says,

> For whom he did foreknow, he also did predestinate to be conformed to the image

of his Son, that he might be the firstborn
among many brethren. (Romans 8:29)

Jesus was chosen as God's plan of man. The Father is the mind of God. The Son lives in me (man), and the Holy Spirit or Ghost changes the brain to think according to the mind. Man becomes born again. This is how we become the children of God. The soul has a mind, and the body has a brain. The spirit is the life in the soul. This life, the spirit of man, is to learn from the Spirit of God—that we are the children of God.

> The Spirit itself beareth witness with our spirit, that we are the children of God. (Romans 8:16)

God's Spirit reveals to our spirit (who then reveals to our mind) that sin is in the brain, and it wants to fight against the thoughts given by God to our minds. It is difficult to understand the difference between the brain and the mind. The brain is of the flesh, and the mind is of the soul, which is the spirit that God has given to the soul. I have a brain, and I have a mind, but it is I who makes the choice.

The Father, the Son, and the Holy Ghost (the mind, the soul, and the brain). It is the Holy Ghost, God, which changes our brains to think with and like our minds.

This is to glorify God!

SOUL, BODY, SPIRIT VERSUS THE FATHER, THE SON. AND THE HOLY GHOST

> A father of the fatherless, and a judge of the widows, is God in his holy habitation.
> —Psalm 68:57 (KJV)

Here the Bible speaks of God as Father.

> Buy to us there is but one God, the Father, of whom are all things, and we in him; and one Lord Jesus Christ, by whom are all things, and we by him. (1 Colossians 8:6, KJV)

Here the Son is shown to be God.

> And we know that the Son of God is come, and hath given us an understanding, that we may know him that is true, and we are in him that is true, even in his Son Jesus Christ. This is the true God, and eternal life. (1 John 5:20, KJV)

Here the Bible says that Jesus Christ, the Son, is God.

In Acts 5:3–4, Satan fills Ananias heart to lie to the Holy Ghost, but the Bible says that he does not lie to man but to God. Here, the Holy Ghost is revealed to be God.

> But Peter said, Ananias, why hath Satan filled thine heart to lie to the Holy Ghost, and to keep back part of the price of the land? Whiles it remained, was it not thine own? And after it was sold, was it not in thine own power? Why hast thou conceived this thing in thine heart? Thou hast not lied unto men, but unto God. (Acts 5:3–4, KJV)

God has a threefold nature which is the Father, the Son, and the Holy Ghost.

These are the three images in which God reveals himself. I believe God is revealing to me that He has a soul, a body, and a spirit that is holy.

> Speak unto all the congregation of the children of Israel, and say unto them, Ye shall be holy: for I the Lord your God am holy. (Leviticus 19:2, KJV)

Here God reveals that he is holy.

> Because it is written, Be ye holy, for I am holy." (1 Peter 1:16, KJV)

What is being shown to me is the Father is the soul of God, the Son is the body of God, and the Spirit of God is the Holy Ghost. They are the threefold nature of God. They are revealed to us as the images of God—the Father, the Son, and the Holy Ghost. The Bible says that we where created in the Image of God. The Bible says in Genesis 1:27 that, "And God said, Let us make man in our image, after our likeness." Here in this verse, the words, *us and our* represents more then one person. This is the threefold nature of God spoken of in this scripture. It is the Soul, the Body, and the Spirit; these are the image of God we are created in. The King James Version of Genesis 1:27 says, "So God created man in his own image, in the image of God created he him; male and female created he them."

We were created to acquire the wisdom, the knowledge, and the understanding that God is teaching us, so that in death, we will become the threefold nature We are to be Christlike. We shall inherit the Spirit of God, The Holy Ghost, who is the guarantee of our inheritance, eternal life.

> And this is the record, that God hath given to us eternal life, and this life is in his Son. (1 John 5:11, KJV)

The soul, the body, and the Holy Ghost versus the Father, the Son and the Holy Ghost.

> For there are three that bear record in heaven, the Father, the Word, and the Holy Ghost: and these three are one. (1 John 5:7, KJV)

This is to glorify God!

SONS OF GOD

> But as many as received him, to them gave he Power to become the Sons of God, even to them that believe on his Name.
> —John 1:12 (KJV)

We, the sinners, are saved through Jesus Christ our Lord and Savior. It is because of God's grace and mercy that the Word became flesh. God revealed his body by being born a man. Christ is the power of God that lives in Jesus, causing Jesus Christ to become the Son of God.

The first of the children of God was Jesus Christ, the only begotten Son of God. The term *only begotten* means one-of-a-kind, a sense captured nicely by the NIV translation, "one and only."

This meaning comes from the *Revell Bible Dictionary*.

It is because of love that God called us to become the sons and daughters of God, the children of God.

> The Spirit itself beareth witness with our spirit, that we are the children of God. (Romans 8:16, KJV)

The Spirit of God is the Holy Ghost, who is the Spirit of truth given to all of the children of God, the sons of God. It is the Spirit of truth that transforms us to become the sons of God. The Holy Ghost delivers the word of God to the children of God according to the will of God. This is how God teaches the sons of God his will. God's will for the sons is to think and act like Christ. We must be willing to change. We must change in order to become like Christ.

> For as many as are led by the Spirit of God, they are the sons of God. (Romans 8:14, KJV)

We are to change the way we think and act and allow the Holy Ghost to lead us according to the will of God. If we do, we will become one of the sons and daughters of God and live forever in heaven and in eternity. This option should really be considered. I would much rather put my faith in Jesus Christ and allow the Holy Ghost to transform me than allow the devil to continue to deceive me, not to become saved or to be a born-again Christian.

> Behold, what manner of Love the Father hath bestowed upon us, that we should be called the sons of God; therefore the world knowth us not, because it knew him not. (1 John 3:1, KJV)

In this scripture we find this question, "What type of love is it that the Father has for us?"

It must be so strong because He wants us to become his children.

This brings about another question, "What must we do to become a child of God?

We must be born of God. We are to die to our will and be reborn of the will of God. We must allow Jesus Christ to become the lord of our life. This is done with faith.

> That if thou shalt confess with thy mouth the Lord Jesus, and shalt believe in thine heart that God hath raised him from the dead, thou shalt be saved. (Romans 10:9, KJV)

But of course, it's just that simple. If you tell Jesus you are a sinner, and you believe in your mind that God brought Jesus back from the dead, you will be saved.

Look at it like this. God came into the world, God died on the cross, and God rose from the grave—these are the three things our God did for us as Jesus Christ our Lord and Savior. The power of God is Christ. The Son of God is our lord. The Holy Ghost is the Spirit of God, our savior.

The reason for the three distinct likenesses is that the Father, the Son and the Holy Ghost are all the same.

They are all God. They are the Trinity, the Godhead, and the Spirit of Truth.

The man is a husband because he has a wife. The same man is a father because he has a child. The same man is also a son because he has parents. Yet the man, whose name is not known, is still the same man.

So is our God the same God as in the past, present, and future?

God is, God was, and God will always be the same God.

> Yet the number of the children of Israel shall be as the sand of the sea, which cannot be measured nor numbered; and it shall come to pass, that in the place where it was said unto them, Ye are not my people, there it shall be said unto them, Ye are the sons of the living God. (Hosea 1:10, KJV)

When we were in darkness, we were not the children or the sons of God—we were sinners. Through God's grace and mercies, God called us out of darkness and into his marvelous light to become the sons of God.

> But ye are a chosen generation, a royal priesthood, an holy nation, a peculiar people; that ye should shew forth the praises of him who hath called you out of darkness into his marvelous light. (1 Peter 2:9, KJV)

We rejoice in praising our God. We long to glorify and lift up the name of Jesus Christ, our Lord and Savior.

> Beloved, now are we the sons of God, and it doth not yet appear what we shall be: but we know that, when he shall appear, we shall be like him; for we shall see him as he is. (1 John 3:2, KJV)

Here the Spirit of God is telling me that here in this world, the world will never see me as Christ, but when Christ returns, I will be just like him and see him.

This is to glorify God

Amen!

STONES OF FIRE REVEALED

> Thou art the anointed cherub that covereth; and I have set thee so: thou wast upon the holy mountain of God; thou hast walked up and down in the midst of the stones of fire.
> —Ezekiel 28:14 (KJV)

These last three words—*stones of fire*—have been brought to my understanding as lava running down a mountain. This <u>was</u> where Satan was, on the holy mountain of God. I believe the mountain had erupted. It is revealed that Satan was a spiritual being, not of the flesh.

How else could he walk up and down the stones of fire?

> Thine heart was lifted up because of thy beauty, thou hast corrupted thy wisdom by reason of thy brightness: I will lay thee before kings, that they may behold thee. (Ezekiel 28:17, KJV)

The brightness is the splendor of a being—a spiritual being. This is why I believe Satan was not physically seen, and that he was walking up and down the stones of fire in spirit so men could not see him. It is possible to be on earth not in physical form, but spiritual.

We are alive in God. We were created as a soul with the Spirit of God that gives us life. The Spirit is life. This life is God within us. It is God who brings us to life. It is by him that we live. Without God, there is no life. Life is not seen, but it is alive just like God is alive and not seen.

> No man hath seen God at any time. If we love one another, God dwelleth in us, and his love is perfected in us. (1 John 4:12, KJV)

This just proves that God is Spirit, and He is alive. God created Satan as a spiritual being, a cherub that covereth. He carried all the risks, the bad things for God. God created him for this very reason.

Through Satan's spirit, he was capable of transforming into what he willed, for he had his own free will to use for the things God commanded him, but he sinned against God.

Because of his sin, God would destroy him from the stones of fire, and God would make him a terror, and Satan would be nothing more than a spirit of terror who lies. Only by his spirit could Satan walk up and down the stones of fire, lava the molten, or fluid rock that issues from a volcano.

(This is the number one verse in the *Random House College Dictionary*.)

This is to glorify God!

THE BRAIN IS CARNAL, THE MIND IS SPIRITUAL

> For to be carnally minded is death; but to be spiritually minded is life and peace.
> —Romans 8:6 (KJV)

The brain is the part born in sin, which makes the brain *carnal*. The brain dies.

> Because the carnal mind is enmity against God: for it is not subject to the law of God, neither indeed can be. (Romans 8:7, KJV)

The mind is the unseen comprehension of the soul brought to life by the Spirit of God. The Bible says man became a living soul, which means that man was able to comprehend.

> I thank God through Jesus Christ our Lord. So then with the mind I myself serve the

law of God; but with the flesh the law of sin.
(Romans 7:25, kjv)

It is revealed that the brain is flesh, and the mind is spiritual. The Bible suggests that we change the way we act and think. This is because there is a difference between the brain and the mind.

The brain is taught by sin to think of carnal matters, and the mind is taught to think spiritually. This is because we have the mind of Christ.

> For who hath known the mind of the Lord, that he may instruct him? But we have the mind of Christ. (1 Corinthians 2:16, kjv)

The Spirit of God speaks to the mind, and the brain fights against the Spirit of God because of sin, which it was born in.

The Bible tells us that the war between God and Satan is fought in the mind, which is a spiritual place.

> Let this mind be in you, which was also in Christ Jesus. (Philippians 2:5)

The mind contains the things of God—spiritual things. The brain receives thoughts of secular things and Satan. It also receives thoughts from the Holy Ghost who talks to the spirit that lives in the mind. The mind is the comprehensive part of our soul. It is here what must change our way of thinking and acting. It is our soul that is to live in eternity with God. Our soul comprehends and lives because of the Spirit of God.

> For we know that the law is spiritual: but I am carnal, sold under sin. (Romans 7:14)

We must learn to let go of sin and learn not to think carnally. The Spirit of God teaches our spirit to think according to the will of God. We must learn the difference between the brain and the mind. We are to let go of our carnality and take hold of our spirituality. The spirituality of this becomes believing with faith and holding on to Christ Jesus. The Bible says in Hebrews 7:16 that Christ is "who is made, not after the law of a carnal commandment, but after the power of an endless life." Here, the power of an endless life is God. Today, Christ lives in the mind of us who have faith in God's promises.

The Holy Ghost makes our mind holy. This is the will of God for our soul. We must change the way we think and act.

This is to glorify God!

THE CROWN OF CREATION

We are consciously alive because of Our Spirit which is the Breath of Life given to us by God Himself.

> And the Lord God formed Man of the dust of the ground, and breathed into his nostrils the Breath of Life; and Man became a living being. (Genesis 2:7)

In Hebrew, the word *ruach* (*breath*) means spirit. By the Spirit is how we know God and the things of God. God is the only one who cannot die. It is for this reason we will live forever. The breath of life from God that lives within us is that which sustains us forever. This breath from God is our Spirit. By its power do our souls live forever. Our soul is the unseen part of us that knows, feels, and chooses.

The choosing part of us comes from our will. Our will is our freedom and responsibility to make a choice. This choice has eternal consequences that determine where we will be in eternity.

> For thus saith the high and lofty One that inhabiteth eternity, whose name is holy; I

> dwell in the high and holy place, with him also that is of a contrite and humble spirit, to revive the spirit of the humble, and to revive the heart of the contrite ones. (Isaiah 57:15)

This scripture is saying that God lives in eternity, and He is the One whose name is holy. He lives in a high and holy place, yet He also lives in us who are sorry for our wrongdoings and have humble spirits. God brings back to life those of us whose spirits are humble and ask from the heart for forgiveness. The soul is the part of yourself that makes you aware of God. It is the spirit that teaches the soul to know God and maintain a personal relationship with God. Your body is to be governed by the soul. Your soul is governed by your spirit, and your spirit is to be governed by God. The Holy Spirit, who is the third person in the Godhead, The Trinity, teaches the human spirit to be aware of the knowledge of God.

> Because that which may be know of God is manifested in them; for God hath showed it unto them. For the invisible things of him from the creation of the world are clearly seen, being understood by the things that are made, even his eternal power and Godhead; so that they are without excuse. (Romans 1:19–20)

God is, God was, and God will always be *God*, the Lofty One that will always inhabit eternity. This knowledge is given to the soul that we might know God. Again, the soul does three things—it knows, it Feels, and it chooses.

Because the body can see, hear, smell, taste, and touch, your body makes your soul aware of the things around you. The soul and spirit cannot do these physical things. This is why they were placed in the body allowing them to be made aware of the physical world around them.

Spiritually, the body helps our soul feel the material world it lives in. Our spirit makes us aware of God's nature that lives in us. It is by our spiritual nature our soul should choose. Our physical nature has been corrupted by the sin that is living in our flesh, in our bodies.

> For when we were in the flesh, the motions of sins, which were by the law, did work in our members to bring forth fruit unto death. (Romans 7:5)

> I thank God through Jesus Christ our Lord. So then with the mind, I myself serve the law of God; but with the flesh the law of sin. (Romans 7:25)

The flesh makes the soul feel selfish desires because sin lies to the spirit. Sin tells the spirit what sin wants to feel.

What sin speaks is a lie.

Sin is controlled by the nature of Satan, who is the father of lies.

> Ye are of your father the devil, and the lust of your father ye will do: he was a murderer from the beginning, and abode not in the truth, because there is no truth in him. When he speaketh a lie, he speaketh of his own: for he is a liar, and the father of it. (John 8:44)

Sin is guided by the lustful desires of Satan, who wants to control your spiritual nature. Satan does not want the Spirit of God to guide your spiritual nature because the Holy Spirit of God is the Truth. This truth gives you the knowledge that you do not have to be a slave to sin.

> But God be thanked, that ye were the servants of sin, but ye have obeyed from the heart that form of doctrine which was delivered you. Being then made free from sin, ye became the servants of righteousness. (Romans 6:17–18)

You, out of your own free will, can choose not to obey sin. The lies of Satan are placed into your spirit so that you would trust these lies that Satan has been telling you all of your life. This is why there is a war within you. The spiritual nature is to be guided by the Holy Spirit of God. Satan controls the sin that controls the flesh that is corrupted. We are to do what our spirit tells us to do. It is by the spirit that we know God. Our spirit tells us what to do. It talks to our soul who makes the choices about what we do and don't do. We make decisions according to the information the spirit tells the soul. Within the soul is our free will of choice. The soul must make the choice to either follow the flesh or the spirit. The key is the Spirit.

> I pray that the glorious Father, the God of our Lord Jesus Christ, would give you a Spirit of wisdom and revelation as you come to know Christ better. The Spirit gives us insight and confidence. Then you will have deeper insight. You will know the confidence that he calls you to have and the glorious wealth that God's people will inherit. You will also know the unlimited greatness of his power as it works with might and strength for us the believers. (Ephesians 1:17)

We, as believers, should allow our Spirit to be guided by The Holy Spirit, not the flesh.

> This Holy Spirit is the guarantee that we will receive our inheritance. We have this guarantee until we are set free to belong to him. God receives praise and glory for this. (Ephesians 1:14)

Our inheritance is the right to live in heaven with God. This is our guarantee that once we die (meaning once we are set free), we will receive the promise of God that we will go to heaven. God is a God of his word. It is best for us to put our trust in the Lord Jesus Christ. It is best for us to be guided by the Holy Spirit, not by the flesh. The flesh feeds the spirit corrupt and negative information from sin controlled by Satan.

At birth, we were born into a world of sin because sin was already in the world. Our bodies were born with sin in the flesh because it is in the flesh of our parents. Sin is in us because all men have sinned.

> So sin came into the world through one person, and death came through sin. Death spread to everyone, because everyone sinned. (Romans 5:12)

As we grow, so does sin. Our spiritual nature lies dormant because our minds have to develop and age according to our bodies which grow from a baby to toddler, and then as an adult. Somewhere in our childhood, we heard the Word of God. Then our spiritual nature began to grow and gain strength.

If we begin to trust in the Lord by faith and ask him to come and live in us as our Lord and Savior, God will save us from sin and death.

He will forgive us and allow us back into His presence through our Lord Jesus Christ. It is by the Holy Spirit that we are transformed, recreated, and born of God.

> Whosoever is born of God doth not commit sin; for his seed remaineth in him; and he cannot sin, because he is born of God. (1 John 3:9)

Now the war begins within our minds. Sin has a head start on influencing the spirit because from child birth, we have received sinful mental stimulation from the world around us. The world of sin plus the sin in our flesh is learned to be trusted. Our flesh cries out for what we want. Like a baby that wants to be fed. The outside world caters to the cry of the flesh by feeding the infant. The baby is quite. The sin in the flesh is satisfied. This is how we learn to trust the sin that lives in us to give us the soul—what we want. We become dependent on sin. Now as we grow we become self-sufficient. We can make choices. Our spiritual nature is still a child, but we are adults who trust sin until the day comes when sin cannot stop the longing we have for God. Then the spirit in us cries to God for help. Because the soul is only used to hearing the lies of sin for help, it almost does not recognize the voice of God. God has sent help by the power of his Holy Spirit through blood and water.

> This is he that came by water and blood, even Jesus Christ; not by water only, but by

water and blood. And it is the Spirit that
beareth witness, because the Spirit is truth.
(1 John 5:6)

His Holy Spirit will guide our spirit according to the will of God who knows the truth of what is best for us, what is best for our soul. Now the soul must make a choice to listen to the corrupt nature or the spiritual nature.

This choice is of eternal consequences,—heaven or hell. Now the soul has a will. It has the power to choose of its own free will.

Meaning it may choose either sin or God.

This choice will determine whether you will live in eternity in damnation (hell) or in paradise (heaven).

For this reason, God has given us our own free will, our right to choose. This choice should be made of our own free will. God has given us the gift of faith. Our faith comes to us by the hearing of the Word of God. The more word the spirit hears from God, the more of a chance it gives the soul to choose correctly. The soul must choose. Whatever it feels the strongest in the spirit will determine how the soul will choose. So for us, it is better to read the Word of God if you want a chance to go to heaven. If we don't read the Word of God, all we are left with is whatever the sin in the world tells our spirit. Plus whatever the sin in our flesh tells us. The lust of the sin of the flesh is what makes a man a homosexual.

> And likewise also the men, leaving the natural use of the woman, burned in their lust one toward another; men with men working that which is unseemly, and receiving in themselves that recompence of their error which was meet. (Romans 1:27)

The soul must choose correctly because for the spirit one force will become more powerful than the other. It all depends on what you feed your spirit the most. What you put in you is what you become.

Think about it, you know right from wrong.

God knows you know.

It is your *choice*. Don't let Satan's lies fool you.

Money, glamour and pride are the characteristics of Satan. Satan's job is to destroy your spiritual nature so you can go to Hell.

> The thief cometh not, but for to steal, and to kill, and to destroy: I am come that they might have life, and that they might have it more abundantly. (John 10:10)

God's promise is the gift of everlasting life. Choose wisely because forever is a long time to be in the wrong place.

This is to glorify God

Amen!

www.ingramcontent.com/pod-product-compliance
Ingram Content Group UK Ltd.
Pitfield, Milton Keynes, MK11 3LW, UK
UKHW022209230426
12048UKWH00016BA/736